Nine Lives of Morris:
Great Tales from One Cool Cat

Stories, Poems and Watercolors
by Morris L. Taylor

Nine Lives of Morris:
Great Tales from One Cool Cat!

Stories and watercolors by Morris L. Taylor
Edited by: Jonathan Taylor
Layout Design: W.E. "Wes" Sanders
Design: Jim Shubin: www.bookalchemist.net

CATALOGING DATA:
Nine Lives of Morris: Great Tales from One Cool Cat!
by: Morris L. Taylor
Memoir—Watercolor—Religion—LGBT—Art—Leather
BDSM—Poetry

ISBN: 978-0-9964390-7-7

Published by A&A Publishers
San Francisco, California
First Edition/First Printing — March 2016
Printed in the United States of America

Nine Lives of Morris:
Great Tales from One Cool Cat

Stories, Poems and Watercolors
by Morris L. Taylor

Montage & Cover Design
by Richard Brooks

Layout Design
byW. E. "Wes" Sander

A&A Publishers
San Francisco, California

SPECIAL THANKS TO:

Linda Watanabe McFerrin, Mentor
Richard Brooks, Montage, Cover
W. E. "Wes" Sander, Layout Design
Jonathan Taylor, Editor, Muse
Lawrence Brown, Financial Advisor

MEMOIR STORIES

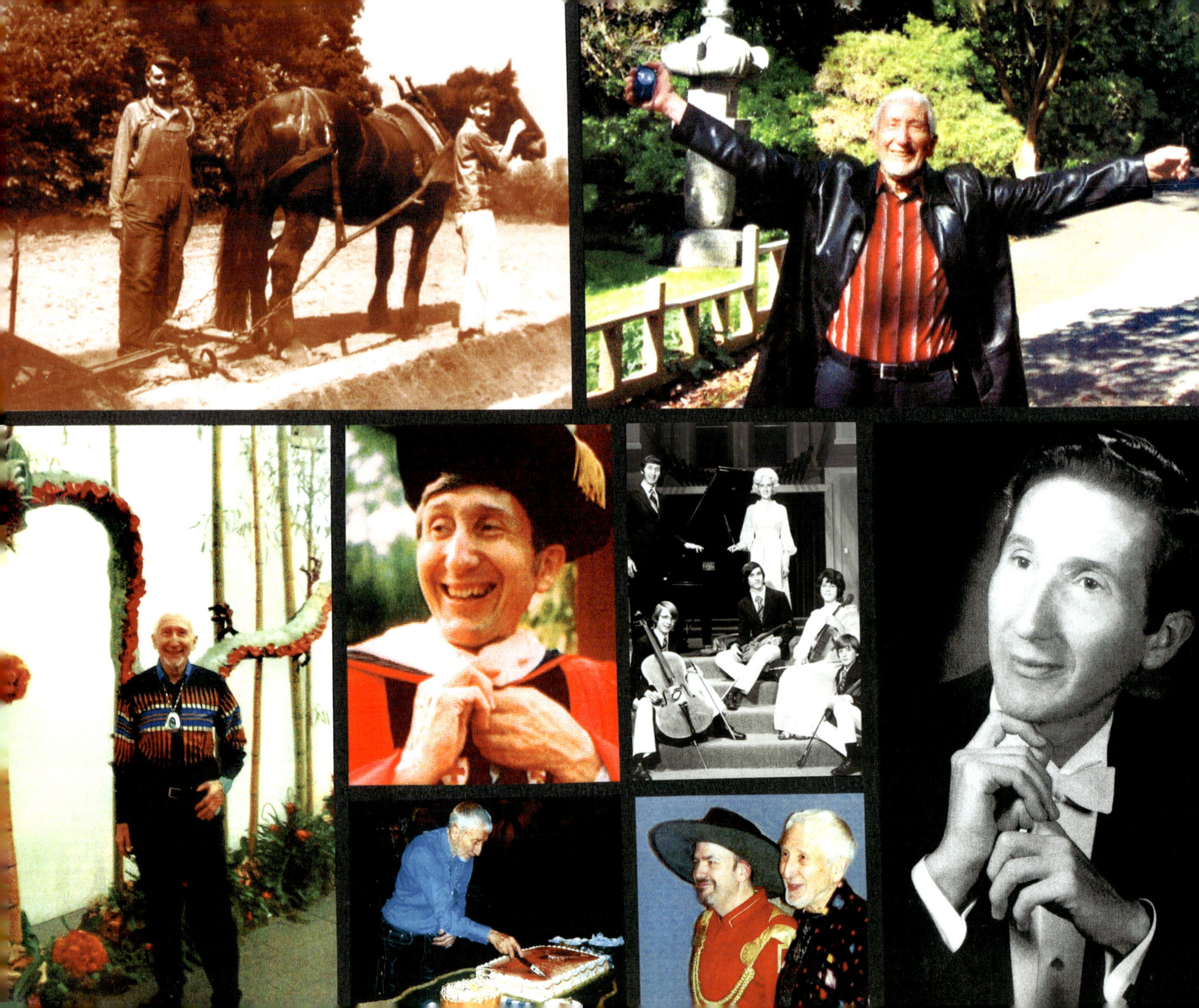

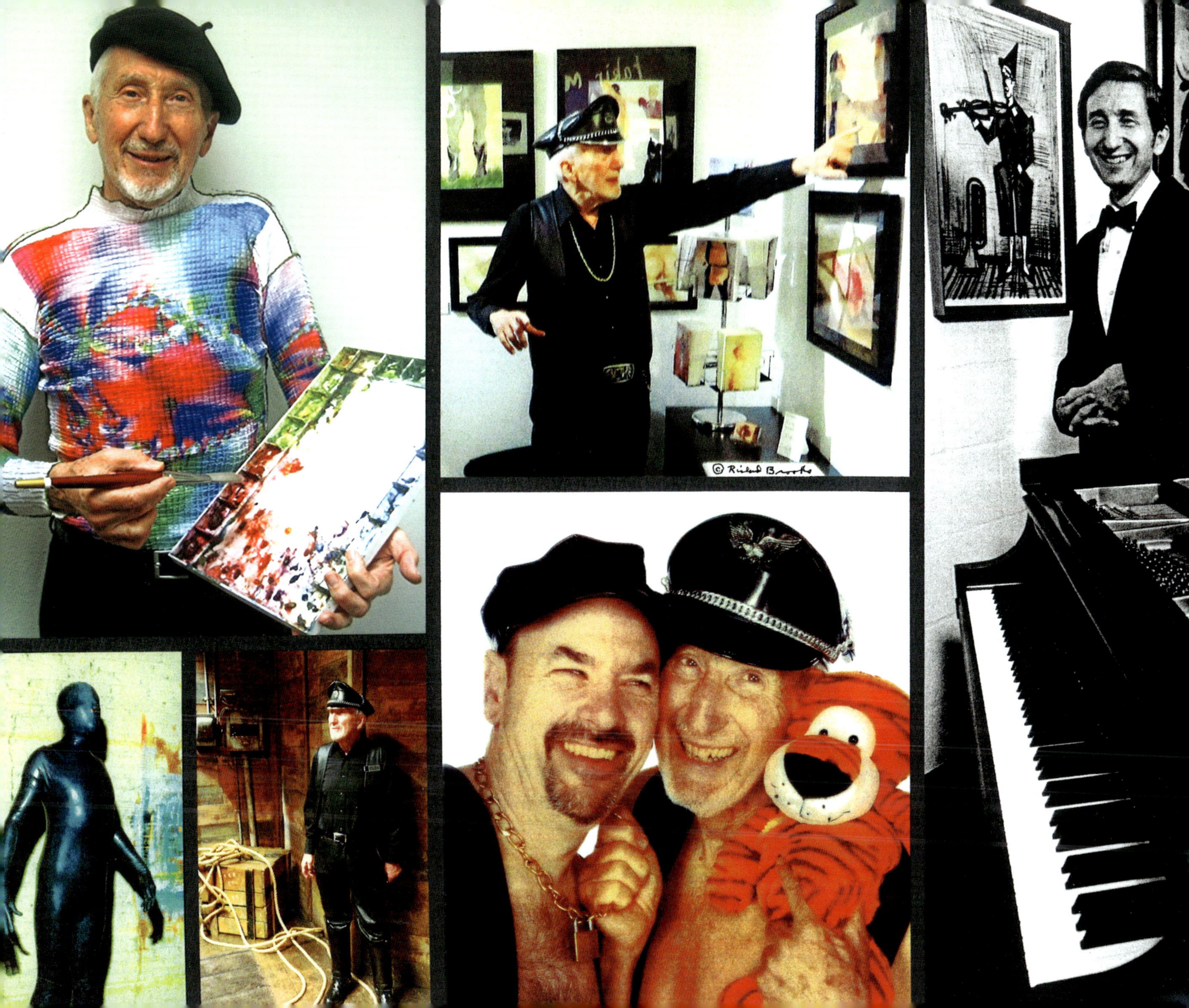
© Richard Brooks

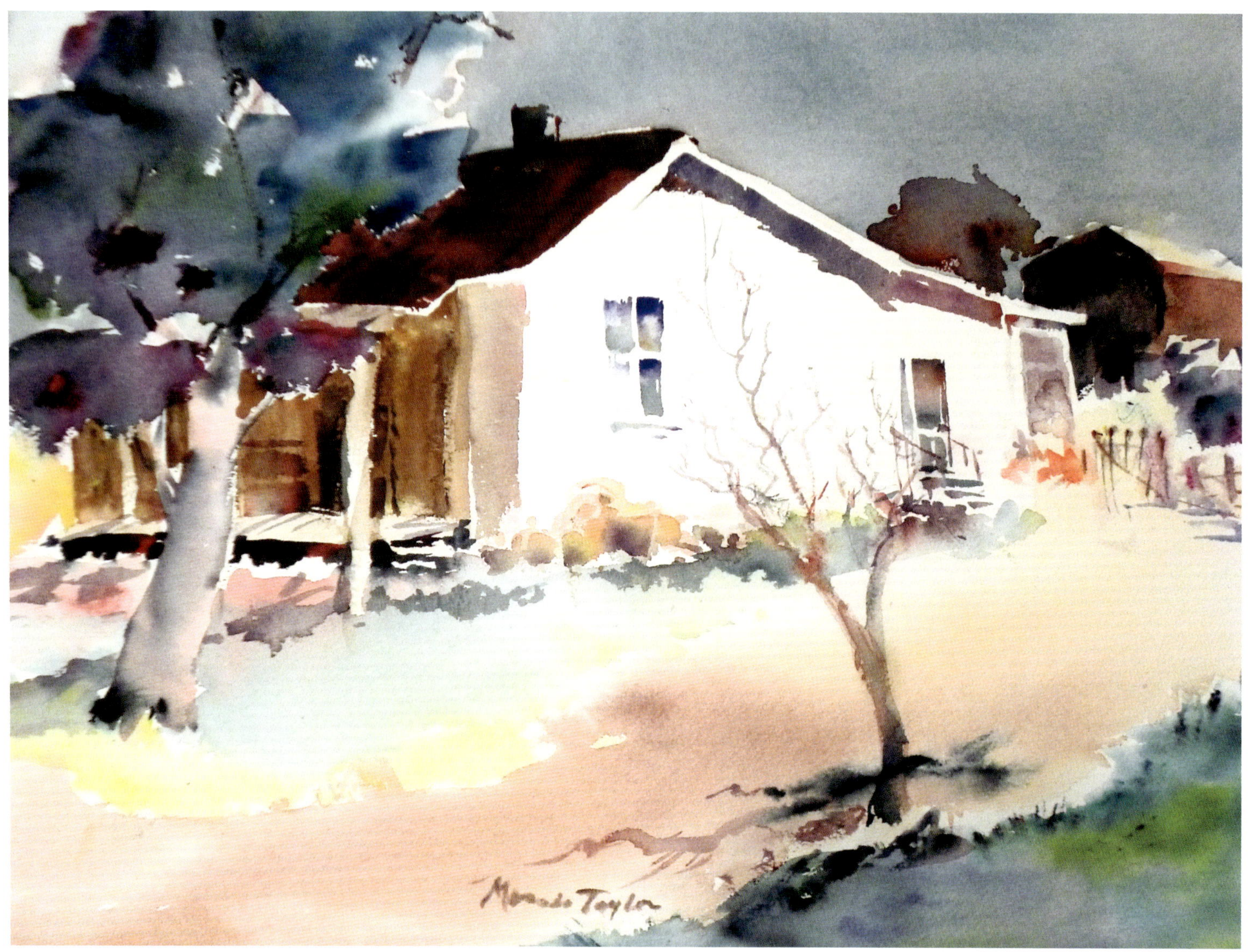

Honeymoon Home, 12x16

THE PILLOW TALKS

I bear the Taylor name. I notice that my four younger siblings have Devlin as their last name. My stepfather, Winfield Devlin, rocks my younger brothers and sister, but not me. I even envy their spankings, but my mother, Alice, says, "Don't you lay a hand on that child," meaning me. I just don't fit into the family.

I suspect that a man named Haywood Taylor is my real dad. In the family register of a Bible bound in brown leather, I see my surname. When I ask my mother Alice about this, I receive only a shrug in return. I have grown to expect this. My mother doesn't hug me, kiss me or tuck me into bed. She shies away from physical touch. She keeps her pain. I keep my silence, but I long to penetrate the mystery that clouds the story of my origin.

When I am in my fifties, Mother comes from Maine to visit me in Michigan. After about a week she decides one day that it is time to be moving on. She hurriedly packs her truck cab and camper shell to the limit with household plants, unkempt clothes and accumulated stuff. We are waving fond goodbyes to signal the end of a week's visit. Suddenly, out of the clear autumn air, an object flies in my direction.

"Here, take this!" she says.

I catch the missile as it hurtles toward my head. "What on earth is this?" I say as I catch a pillow.

My mother mischievously gives an enigmatic clue. "My boyfriends are fighting in there," she says. Without a parting hug, she leaps into the Dodge Ram and steps on the gas.

I shout after her, "Let me know when you get there." I'm not sure where "there" is or how she will let me know. That's my mom, wandering like a nomad. Will she ever settle down?

Real artifacts of my mother's life are few; there's lots of junk but not much of value or sentiment. So I treasure this heart-shaped pillow in green organza trimmed with lace. The pink floral embroidery is a creation of her more youthful hands.

While enjoying the blazing fireplace at Christmas time, my wife, Rilla, says to me, "I dare you to find out what is in the pillow."

Like my name-alike, Morris the Cat, curiosity gets the better of me. "Okay. How can we get inside?" I finally say to Rilla.

"Bring me the sewing box," she replies. "You'll find a seam ripper in there."

The musty goose feathers fly into the atmosphere sending me into a fit of sneezing. Then my fingers feel pieces of paper confetti, the size of my little fingernail.

"I have a hunch." I say. "Maybe this will lead to the mystery of my father's identity."

First we separate the feathers from the paper fragments. Patiently Rilla and I sort the random, enigmatic pile of torn letters. Then we hit upon a scheme worthy of Agatha Christie's detective, Hercule Poirot. We sort through the paper fragments, focusing on two features: postmarks and ink signatures. Without interlocking guides or color cues, we assemble pieces into crossword-like puzzles.

"I've found it!" exclaims Rilla. "The same town seems to be on several postmarks, Williamsburg, Kentucky. I can't quite make out the date, but I think it is 1930."

"I was born in January of 1931. That's the clue I've been looking for all my life. The area around there must be the place where my father lived." I have a vague childhood memory from Mrs. Hartwell, an old family friend. She said Mom had met and married a coastguardsman in New London, Connecticut, and that he hailed from down south in Appalachia.

By spring I have almost forgotten the pillow, but Rilla is hot on the trail. As she is driving from our home in Buchanan, Michigan, to a professional meeting near Chattanooga, Tennessee, she deliberately stops to fill her tank with gas in Williamsburg near Interstate 75. "You know anybody around here with the last name of Taylor; Haywood, or maybe Hayward, Taylor?" she asks the service station attendant.

"Lady, there's a bunch of them Taylors. All up and down these valleys to the west," says the guy at the pump.

So the hunt begins in earnest. Skillful sleuthing uncovers Taylors who are relatives of mine. Rilla returns home with pictures: a primitive Baptist Church where my pa taught Sunday school and a bare wood house with a tin roof built by my grandpa. Most valued of all is an image of Haywood standing next to my Uncle Dee, who is strumming on the banjo. Another yellowed photo shows my pa and his six brothers at Grandma Taylor's funeral.

A few months later I decide that I have to meet my kinfolk. My wife and I drive to Jellico, Tennessee, to meet a second cousin named Glenda who joins us in the adventure. On the Fourth of July we three head north over the nearby state line into Kentucky, through Williamsburg, and then west until the tarred road ends. Another few miles along the dirt road, Glenda stops the car and winds down the window. All I can hear is a chorus of howling coon dogs. Glenda shouts upward toward the porch, "Am them thar' bitin' dawgs?"

We are not expected. A few shouted questions and answers, back and forth, overcome suspicions about meeting up with strangers. "Come on up," says a wizened lady with her hair in a bun, a flowered apron over her calico dress.

We climb up the tricky toeholds indented into the clay embankment. The rocking chairs on the porch move with excitement as we brush by them. Aunt Mae calls off the dogs with mock swats. I hand a box of chocolates around. When Mae eagerly nibbles her favorite crème, I notice her remaining teeth are stained from chewing tobacco. In the curtained room I see a skin-and-bones man with dark, searching eyes. Mae introduces me to Uncle Dee. He props himself up on a straw-filled mattress covered with a fresh white sheet. Mae explains that his speech is impaired from a stroke a few years back, but I sense that my uncle is eager to talk.

Aunt Mae unfolds the story of my origins. "Your dad was in the Coast Guard somewhere up north. At the submarine base, I reckon."

"New London is the city on my birth certificate. How did he meet my mother, Alice?" I ask.

"Alice was sixteen or seventeen when she met Haywood at the beach."

"Her father was a minister. I don't think he would have approved of his little girl going to the beach alone," I say.

"Haywood and Alice were married in Jellico, Tennessee." Mae continues. "The two of them walked across the mountains into Kentucky. They lived in an unpainted cabin with a tin roof. You can almost see it, right down this road apiece. Those days, menfolk expected their women to split wood, scrub the porch and slop hogs. Still do, I reckon."

"That kind of life must have been a lot different from the sheltered life Alice had at home," I chime in.

Aunt Mae continues the story. "Your mother and I used to walk about ten miles to the nearest country store to get some supplies and pick up the mail. On one of these treks, Alice sneaked a letter to her pa asking him to come get her." Mae adds, "Your grandpa came with the county sheriff to this very house with a warrant demanding the release of Alice."

At the height of the depression my grandpa was laid off from his preaching assignments. He spent his last money on a Greyhound bus ticket to rescue his daughter, my mother Alice.

The quest to find my father is validated by two words. My blood uncle, the last of six brothers of my now deceased father, utters with obvious strain, "German. Preacher." My grandfather Freiberger was both.

Alas! Pa died before I met him. Some time later I attend the burial of another uncle, Leonard. Each mourner rides in solemn procession from the funeral home in Williamsburg, to the country church. My newly found brother, Howard Joe, insists we drive the twenty miles slowly, stopping by all the meaningful places along the mostly dirt road to the cemetery. Relatives say, "This affair is the spitting image of your pa's funeral." The same soprano sings "Amazing Grace" with a nasal twang. The same preacher intones the eulogy. At my father's gravesite, I mourn the passing of my biological daddy, Haywood Taylor.

You who knew my dad,
please speak to me
for I'm curious;
I want to know him too.

These are the hills he wandered,
the valley where my father chose to live
amidst indigo bunting, holly and pine
along the path to the spring.

See the family resemblance.
I need to sit by this stream
to be where you are
'cause I'm sure Daddy loves me.

HEIRLOOM TOMATOES FROM THE PIGSTY

In Massachusetts during the late 1930's folks like us are still affected by the Great Depression. Hungry as we children feel, my mother is generous and gives away produce from our country garden to city relatives.

In New England gardens, varicolored tomatoes of different shapes and sizes are common long before the designation "Heirloom," even before they were called "Heritage" in England. Our tomatoes are organic. Under each seedling we place a half shovel of chicken droppings mixed with compost.

As a boy of eight I envy large, firm tomatoes pictured on the Burpee seed packages I sell to make pin money. Their uniform size and color are similar to the tomatoes sold in the Atlantic & Pacific market and on rural fruit stands. What would it be like to slice these smooth vegetables? Oh, I know that argument; they may be fruits. In my house the choice is whether to put salt or sugar on the fragrant, juicy slices.

I think to myself, *How do our neighbors get large, red tomatoes to grow in their garden?* They always seem to have the first ripe ones of the season. When I pass by their tomato patch, the vines are neatly staked in rows. Two or three stalks grow up the poles as high as a man's head, with tomatoes in various stages of ripening.

A kid believes his mother knows everything, so I ask,

"How come their tomatoes are so great?"

"The Joneses have money to buy maturing hothouse plants already in blossom. This gives their tomato plants a head start of several weeks," she replies.

"What's a hothouse?"

"It's like the Moreschi brothers have for their flowers. A coal burning stove heats the glass greenhouses."

I can identify with that answer because many times I go with my grandfather to Shrewsbury, Massachusetts, delivering gladiolas to the Moreschi florist business. From these Italian friends I learn to pluck the suckers, small shoots that sap energy from the ripening tomatoes. With a twinge of envy I say, "The neighbors think they are so smart just because they can afford hothouse tomato plants. That's okay, Mom. Ours taste better."

"Morris, you just wait. When the danger of frost is over, we'll get some tomato plants for free. The Tambolli brothers, garbage collectors from neighboring Clinton, have given us permission to dig all the tomato plants we want."

A couple of weeks later, with a spade and boxes rattling in the wheelbarrow, Mom and I tromp a half mile up the road to get our freebies. I admit there is an acrid stink in the pigsty, and some muddy sow and piglet tracks too, but the tomato plants look lush this year. They have grown from tomato seeds in the swill fed to the swine last year.

We eagerly dig the healthiest and tallest ones. The load seems heavy because I am ordered to leave a clump of fertile dirt on the tender roots. "To make them grow better," Mom says.

We have another option. When one particular tomato appeals to our taste, Mother will carefully let the choice fruit ripen fully and save the seeds for another season. The next spring I plant these special seeds in a box that sits on a sunny windowsill. When the seedlings are two to four inches tall, they are ready for transplanting into an outdoor hotbed.

I help construct our hotbed by digging a shallow, rectangular hole that I fill with a mix of old manure and last year's wormy compost. After raking the surface soil into fine and smooth condition, I replant the coveted tomato seedlings in a grid. Then I punch the soil with my bare fist to get rid of air bubbles. A frame of old lumber rims the enclosure that is topped with a secondhand window sash. Through the glass the rays of the spring sun are magnified to warm the seedlings from above, while the manure warms the roots from beneath. On brilliant days I remember to prop open the window to provide ventilation.

All summer long our tomatoes have color: bright orange, mahogany-green, golden-yellow as well as traditional reds. The various sizes and shapes provide an array of mouth-watering flavors. Long before organic or heirloom tomatoes become popular and expensive, I know what juicy, luscious and gorgeous tomatoes are available by natural selection from the swill and the discarded tomatoes now growing in the neighbor's old pigpens.

Oh, one last trick. In autumn, just before the first killing frost, I pull the mature vines. I hang them by the roots on a nail from the floor joists. Each plant extends downward to the floor of the basement. The sap from the vines gradually ripens the developing tomatoes. After the holiday season we depend upon the bottled tomatoes mother and I have preserved over a wood fire in a huge copper boiler.

As we enjoy these fabulous tomatoes fresh from the garden or bottled in canning jars, Mother says, "This is the poor man's orange."

If we are fortunate, the family eats heirloom tomatoes until Christmas.

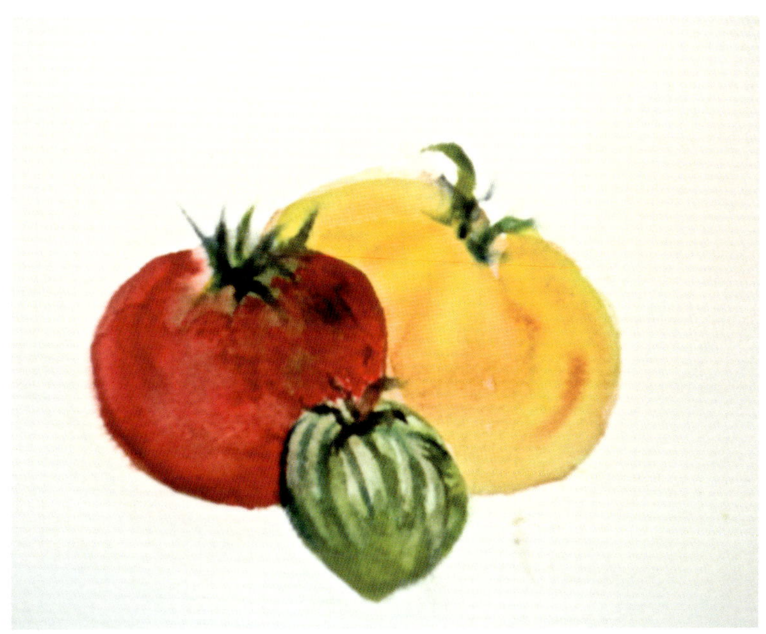

Heirloom Tomatoes, 5 x 6

Marion L. Taylor

MY KALEIDOSCOPES

Squint one eye.
    Iridescent tints of a dragon fly.

Hold it just right.
    Blazing and brilliant hues ignite.

Tilt toward the light.
    Radiating borealis of winter's night.

Can't hold it steady?
    Changing mosaics of colored confetti.

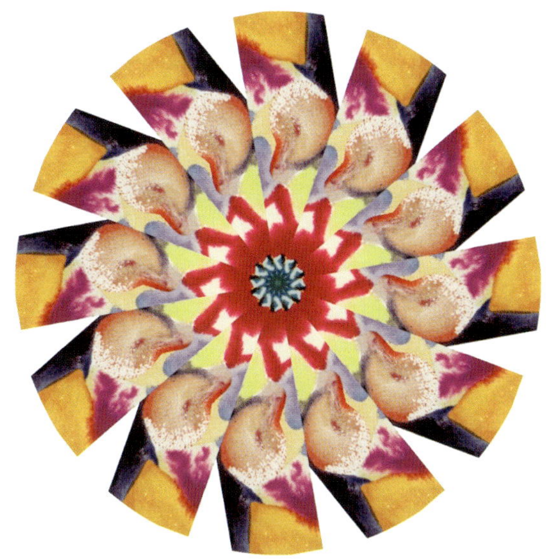

Jiggle a bit.
    Precious jewels multi-facedly lit.

New patterns seek.
    Chandelier prism or flamboyant antique.

Point toward the fire.
    Phosphorescent El Greco admire.

Spin the two wheels.
    A resplendent refraction reveals.

THAT'S WHY EVERYONE HOPES
TO PLAY WITH MY KALEIDOSCOPES.

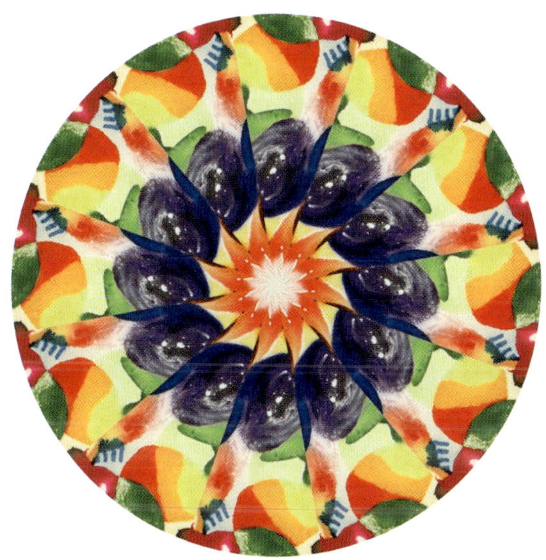

◀ *Kaleidoscopic Sampler, 9x12*

FALLING INTO LINE

As a young child I only see my mother summers and some holidays; she has a new husband, Winfield Devlin, and they have two children—my half-brother Skippy, and half-sister Marie. It is the early 1930s. They are poor.

Pa and Ma Sward lead the family that I most identify with during my early childhood. They live in East Braintree, Massachusetts. This Swedish family takes me into their home out to the kindness of their hearts. Ma Sward and her daughter, Marie, are converts to Seventh-day Adventism from my Grandfather Freiberger's evangelism. My Mother Alice used to play the piano for the hymns at his tent meetings. Ida Sward has a gentle voice and a kind glance. She wears a faded dress. Her stockings are knee high, held there by a twisted knot. She is always busy doing things like making food in the large kitchen, ironing on her mangle or tidying up the house.

Oscar Sward is retired, kind of rough and gruff. He has a small room at the top of the stairs where he spends most of his time. I pass by his door, which is usually shut, but I know he is in there from the pungent smell of his pipe smoke.

Marie, the oldest daughter, is a severe but kindly spinster lady. I sleep in her bed. One night I wake up under the bed and climb back up. At age four and a half I begin the first grade at Manatequot, a public school where Marie Sward teaches. Then I skip a grade.

I really like George, an adult bachelor. His room seems larger, and he has a radio on a table close to his bed. Adventist household radios only play the news. But I sneak into George's room to listen to forbidden, scary stories late at night before he comes home from his bachelors' parties. His favorite weekend radio programs are ballgames and Swedish polkas, during which time I love to jump on his body as he lies on a day couch in the dining room.

The Swards live in a two-story house situated on a large corner lot, 130 East Hayward Street. I cut the scraggly lawn with a push lawn mower that I can barely reach. A privet hedge surrounds the property, and I trim it sometimes with a hand clipper that I can scarcely lift. The Sward's living room is dominated by a tall, upright piano. Someone teaches me how to play "Chopsticks." I am a real nuisance playing the doggerel music over and over, improvising new variations to go with the repetitive bass chords. On the music rack of the piano I spy a hymnal, *Christ in Song*. I pick out tunes by ear until they sound like the hymns at church and the music in front of me. Gradually I figure out on my own what most of the notation means.

Folks say that I am a musical kid, because as a boy soprano, I like to sing. When an adult has time to teach me a song, I am sure to be "up front" at Sabbath School, church worship, evangelistic meetings or sometimes as soloist on the radio.

At Christmas time the Sward family festoons a fragrant Christmas tree with bright trimmings. Even though I am not part of the biological family, there are presents for me, a child of seven years. When it is my turn, I sit in the middle of the room to open the packages. The adults tease, "You're all thumbs."

"Okay," I say, "Let's hear you say that when you play with my present: Pick Up Sticks." My steady little hand almost always wins.

The best present that year is a knickers suit for me to wear to church. The baggy pants with tight elastic binding hold the breeches just below my kneecaps. They itch all the time. Long socks cover my legs from knee to toe. The outfit is topped with a white shirt and a necktie, which I can tie by myself.

That same year I become excited about making things with a needle and thread. I design items using scraps from Ma Sward's sewing basket. With two knitting needles I fashion a fabric of orange colored yarn. This pouch I baste with needle and thread and line with white silk. I invent a way to install a zipper and attach a handle. When I cheerfully show my creation, both kids and adults laugh. I cry and hide the purse. My self-image is so crushed that I angrily destroy all my handiwork beyond recognition and vow to do no more girlish things.

When I am eight years old, Pa Sward and two of his grown sons decide that I need to be encouraged to do boyish activities. Over the objection of the ladies, the guys take me ice fishing. Despite a new dusting of snow, the early spring thaw is nipping at the heels of winter. I am scared of falling into the icy cold water since I cannot swim.

"Stay close to me, ya hear!" says Oscar. "I don't want you to get in the way of setting the traps."

I hold onto his pant leg and attempt to keep up with his stride over the frozen surface. I watch as the men chisel five round holes and attach lines with hooks to the stakes hammered into the ice. When the fish nibble the bait, a trap-like mechanism causes a red flag to spring up where it can be seen from a distance. The fisherman rushes to reel in the catch.

Suddenly I feel my left foot sink into a crack. Water fills my shoe, wets my pants and seeps into my crotch. I yell, "Help! I'm falling in."

"Grab my hand. Why did you go and do that? Our traps are not fully baited," grumbles Pa Sward.

"It's not my fault. I was hanging on to you when I broke the ice," I complain.

Pointing toward the shore, Oscar says, "I knew you would be a nuisance. There. Take these matches and go make a fire."

Terrified of falling in again, I lie on my stomach, and begin to crawl carefully toward the distant shore. The sun gradually bursts through the haze. I can see more clearly where the cracks are dangerous. As I nearly reach land, the ice gives way. I stumble over the grasses and reeds that line the bank. I gather hands full of dry vegetation for tinder, and I find a cardboard box and a few dry sticks for fuel. I like to make fire. I warm my freezing cold hands and feet, and I gradually dry my clothes. I vow never to go ice fishing again.

THE SECRET BLUEBERRY PATCH

"You better climb up to bed," my mother warns. "Three in the morning is awful early."

"Where are we going?" I ask.

"That's none of your business." Seeing my anxious face, she adds, "We're going to pick blueberries."

I am living in Lancaster, Massachusetts with my mother for the summer, so my half siblings, younger than I, are in on the trip. In the wee hours, I hear my grandfather's old Model T pull into our driveway. Mother and my sister, Marie, sit in the cab with my grandpa driving. My brother, Skippy, and I scramble into the open-air bed of the truck. We huddle under a blanket close to the front. The buckets and pails rattle.

Daylight is dawning as we pull off the tarred road and head up the slope of a mountain in southern New Hampshire. The ruts become deeper as we approach a swampy area. Half asleep, I am jerked awake. "Ouch," I yell. "What's going on? Did we break an axle?"

Mom rolls down her window and shouts, "It's only a corduroy road." When we get to a smooth place, she explains, "That's the way you get across the squishy swamp. Loggers lay down the slabs from the saw mill."

"I get it. The flat part is down and the curved part is up," I say.

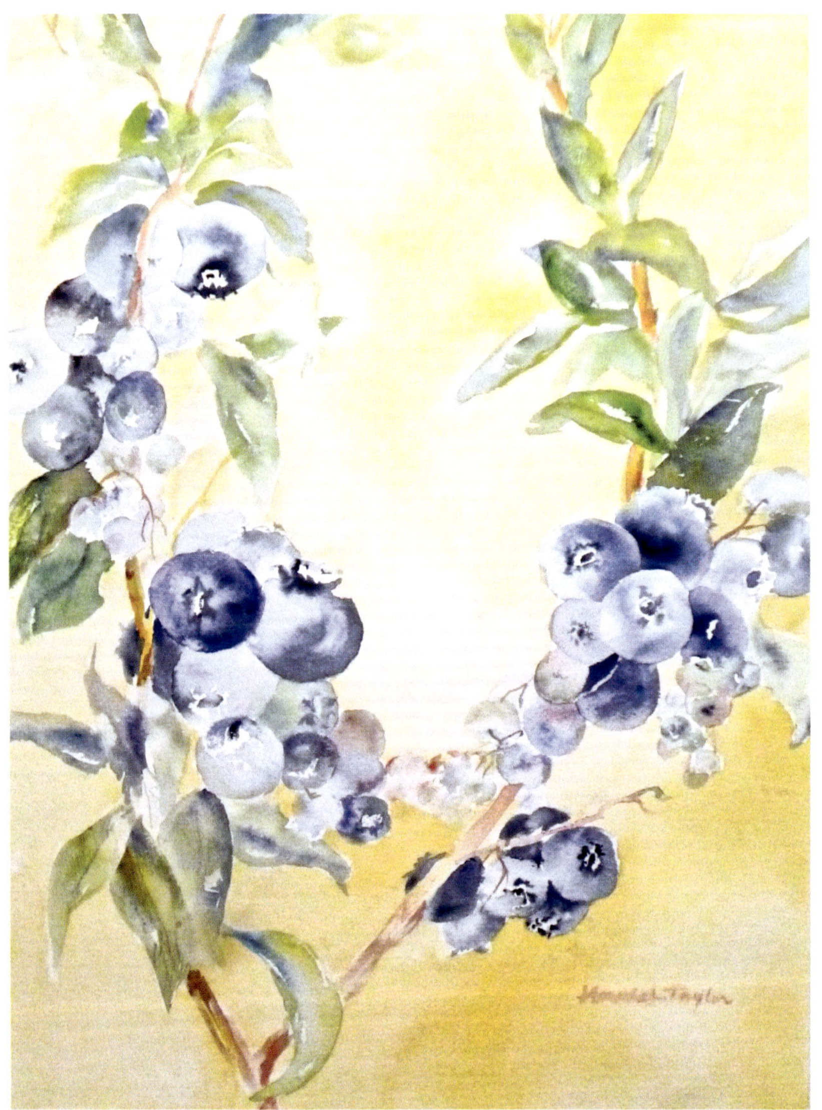

Picking Blueberries, 16x12

"That's as far as we can drive on this abandoned road," announces Grandpy. "Grab some pails and the lunch."

The path grows steeper. Wet grass soaks my pants. Spider webs glisten in the slowly rising sun. "How much farther?" I complain.

"We're almost there. And I want you to stop talking. Nobody should know where we're going," warns Grandpy.

"Yes, and don't you dare start eating berries," adds Mother. "You can have all you want later, but in the field you only put them in your bucket."

The low bush berries are ripe near the exposed rocks. My nimble fingers of both hands milk the blue globes. "Come over here." I beckon my mother. "Mine are bigger!"

"Shh. Be quiet. Just pick."

Without even looking into the bucket attached to my waist belt, I plop handfuls of berries into the opening. I have cut the lid off a gallon can, punched two holes with a nail and bent a wire to form a handle. Soon the bottom is covered, then the bucket is half-full, and in an hour I can hardly walk with the weight.

"Empty them into the big pail," says Grandpy. Then he camouflages the stash where only he can find it again.

"Come over here, Skippy," I shout.

Another impatient "Shh. I told you to be quiet."

"I'm scared. What is this creature on that low branch?" I whisper.

"Don't touch it! That's a porcupine," says Skippy.

"You're right," I say. "I remember the night our dog got quills in his nose. I can still hear the yelps when Grandpy pulled those horrible barbs with pliers."

Before noon all the containers we've brought are overflowing. My grandpa attaches two gallon buckets to his waist belt. Two over-the-shoulder straps hold larger milk pails. The largest containers are in his hands. He looks like a packhorse.

"Can I help carry?"

"No, you might stumble. The berries are impossible to pick out of the grass."

"Oh, let him," says Mother.

I proudly carry two smaller containers.

This July is a particularly good season; our total loot is between ninety and a hundred quarts of blueberries. On the way home we sell enough berries to buy some sugar and jar lids for canning.

Our blue tongues and stained teeth attest to the fact that my brother and I have no muzzle on the way home. My teeth crush the blueberries. My blue saliva craves the acidic sweetness. When I close my eyes, I see the blue globules dance. I dream warm pie and juicy cobbler.

Seventy plus years later, I still do not know where that secret blueberry patch is located.

MOM'S FANCY WORK

Mom's fingers fly swiftly. The thread wraps around the index fingers of her left hand to keep the tension just right. With her other hand she deftly handles the crochet hook.

One day I ask her, "How come you're always making fancy work?"

Looking over her drugstore glasses, she says, "These are my cigarettes and booze."

Mom personifies the adage, "The Devil finds work for idle hands." Despite her name, Alice Mae Devlin, there is no devil in her hands. I know. She keeps hers busy, and mine, too.

"Here, Morris, is the box of fancy work. Sell what you can along the way to the grocery store and bring back some food."

So off I trudge down the roads of Lancaster, Massachusetts, taking care to keep the box level in my outstretched arms. To a nine-year-old boy every house has a monster behind the door. Finally I get up my courage and knock. "No thank you, son," the woman who appears says as she smiles.

I keep trying. My arms begin to ache as the summer sun mocks me. There is no motivation like hunger. Out of need or pity, I will never know, one lady just raves over the baby booties. She takes her time choosing the color. "Maybe it's a boy or maybe a girl," she wonders aloud. "I'll take the pair with the green ribbon." And when she pays me, she brings a drink of juice and a cookie.

Just how far down the list will two dollars go? The can of beans and a loaf of bread are secure. I've got to keep trying to sell. I know how much Mom likes the flavor of butter.

I skip the house with the growling dog. Timidly, I rap on the blue door of the next house. From the lacy curtains I can tell someone there might have money to buy. An older lady, rag curlers in her lavender hair and a gauzy dressing gown draped over her stooped body, opens the door.

"Come right in. What do you have in that box?"

I clumsily remove the tattered cover and part the rustling tissue paper. I take out one of the ecru curtain pulls. The six-pointed star shape is accented by a blue bead that matches the blue of her drapes. My boyish salesmanship takes it up a notch. I hold it up to her window shades. The motes in the sunbeam accentuate the ecru color of her curtains.

"You say they are fifty cents each. How much for all eight of them?" she inquires.

In my excitement I answer, "Five dollars, Ma'am." Then I quickly realize my mistake. "Sorry, I mean four dollars."

"Here's the five. I reckon you will use it wisely."

I am sweaty and out of breath. But I do manage to say, "Thank you very, very much." That day I proudly walk home with all the groceries on the list including the quarter pound of butter.

Postscript: To this day, every child and grandchild has an afghan that Mother Alice crocheted, largely from the wool of unraveled sweaters from a second hand store.

WORLD WAR II AND CHILDHOOD

Remember Pearl Harbor, December 7, 1941?

I do.

Now I live in Lancaster, Massachusetts, with my mother, stepfather, and three half siblings— Skippy, Marie and Jimmy. This is the first time I live year round with Winfield Devlin, an army man of nine years and now an automotive mechanic.

I am ten years old and in the sixth grade at Browning Memorial Elementary School. When Japan enters the war, there is a deep hush. Air is vacuumed out of the atmosphere. I see the look of concern on adult faces.

Our teacher, Euphemia Bryan, tells my class that times are serious. "This may be Armageddon, the final battle signaling the end of the world. According to the *Book of Revelation in the Bible,* Jesus will soon return to earth. The wicked will go to hell; the saints shall rise to be with our Lord in heaven."

My child mind immediately focuses on the hand-painted cloth charts that my Grandfather Freiberger uses in his evangelistic meetings. The beasts and images frighten me. At night I get nightmares about the prophetic war carnage. Even in the daytime I see visions of the Second Coming of Christ dance before my eyes.

On the west coast of the United States, Japanese submarines are caught sneaking into the San Francisco Estuary. On the east coast, where I live, people are afraid of bombers entering our airspace. A brownout means that all curtains are to be drawn with no light escaping. A blackout demands that no lights are permitted, not even a cigarette.

Speaking of cigarettes, my stepfather smokes. This luxury and some necessities are being rationed. With our large family we have coupons to spare, like for shoes. Our large family does not have the money to buy them, so I am wearing secondhand shoes that require a new piece of cardboard every morning. Our garden is no victory garden; our acre patch provides necessary seasonal food. The excess vegetables we bottle in jars with our copper kettle, which holds twenty-six quarts at a time.

My mother trades ration coupons for things we need, except for butter, Mom's one extravagance. One Friday in January, she stands in the breezy alley way clad in an old raccoon coat waiting for the butter store to open. Her oversized coat hides the fact that she is pregnant. As an accessory necessary to get another portion of butter, I also stand in line at seven in the morning. I shiver, clutching an old airman's coat with a fur-trimmed hood. As usual, Mom is crocheting as she gossips with the other people.

The next Monday, the ladies get up the courage to ask, "Didn't we read in the *Clinton Daily Item* that Alice Devlin is the proud mother of a baby boy?"

Without a pause comes the retort, "I told you that what I was knitting' ain't for Britain."

The ladies chuckle, for many of them and their friends do knit bandages for wounded American and

British soldiers.

"Yeah," I add proudly. "That's my new brother Bobby."

My family and I are living on Shirley Road, in Lancaster, Massachusetts, on the edge of a military base. With hurried mobilization of troops, Fort Devens, where my stepfather repairs military vehicles in the motor pool, becomes an induction and training center for army recruits.

As the troop levels rise, so does the need for barracks and training grounds. My parents receive a notice saying that the United States Government will seize our property by eminent domain. Our house is partially finished with only a tarred paper exterior, but it is a roof over the heads of four siblings, my mother and stepfather and me.

The summons arrives. The offer? Eight thousand dollars with a thirty-day notice to vacate the premises. When we object, the representative says the government will move everything we own to the property line within thirty days unless our house is already empty. My parents have no savings. They borrow money at high interest, which puts them further into financial stress.

Housing is in great demand. As more men are inducted into the army, they arrive by train and bus for high-intensity maneuvers. During these tense two months of basic training, sweethearts and family want to live nearby to spend a few last weekends together before shipping across the submarine-infested waters of the North Atlantic.

My mother drives to nearby Clinton. Finally, she finds one flat available at exorbitant rent. "I'll pay. Here is the deposit," she says.

The landlady takes the money and casually announces, "Of course, you do not have any children or pets."

"I have four children and a new baby," my mother replies.

"Well, you can't move in here."

"Just a minute, lady. I'll go home and shoot them," Mom says. "I'll be right back."

"Oh, no. Don't do that," gasps the woman, but she does not budge. "No children. No pets."

A triple whammy—no place to live, my stepfather loses his job, and no advance on the property. My stepdad becomes ill from carbon monoxide in the enclosed and unventilated garage where he works. The seven of us travel with a few possessions to a town just over the border from Charlton, Massachusetts, into rural Connecticut. We stay with relatives, and then our family moves into an abandoned sawmill.

At first it seems like a vacation. In summer there is plenty of space to play outdoors, sawdust piles to jump into and a dammed-up creek for swimming. At night the whippoorwills keep us awake. They come close to our windows, hit their beaks on a log, then let out this penetrating call: a high pitched "whip," a short low "poor," and a medium sounding "will."

After a while the fun fades. We discover that the owners of the sawmill do not like kids spreading the sawdust around. The watering hole is infested with poisonous water moccasins. Then one day my brother

Bobby is carrying drinking water from a distant well in a glass jar. He trips and falls, severing the arteries of his wrist. My mother wraps a tight piece of cloth and takes off running with Bobby in her arms. It is almost a mile to the nearest house. A neighbor drives both of them in a car to the nearest doctor, eight miles further down a mostly dirt road. My brother nearly bleeds to death, but the doctor saves his life by a tourniquet, stitches and a blood transfusion.

A few weeks after we move to Connecticut, all of us kids are sequestered in a relative's living room. The shades are drawn. I smell the musty furniture and choke on the dust of the parlor, a room rarely used. Something seems eerie in the way the adults shoo us out of sight and sound. I am the oldest, and I finally figure out what's happening. A cousin has had the good luck of bagging a five-point buck. It is not deer hunting season, and the family cannot afford the license anyway. So the adults must make sure that no tattletale kids are going to rat on killing this deer for food without a proper license and out of season.

These country folk are strict Sunday keepers. What the church lacks in formal liturgy or fancy architecture, they make up for in preaching zeal and gospel singing. I am precocious for my age. I am put up front on the rostrum to recite, in order, the names of the sixty-six books of the *King James Bible*. Sometimes I repeat, by heart, a poem about Potiphar's wife who had a dream she told to the Roman counsel with a warning not to convict Jesus, the Jewish Messiah. There are lots of arguments about religion. Although my mother is not pious, she can out-argue them all.

Before the winter arrives my family moves back to Lancaster, Massachusetts, where we live in the cellar hole of an unfinished house. The floor joists, what would have been the first floor level, are covered with tarred paper. A rickety pair of stairs leads into the basement that has a concrete floor. The windows are horizontal above the dirt grade. A stovepipe juts above the ground level. I think of 1942 as the dark winter. The war seems far away. As poor as we are, my mother buys twenty-five cent stamps that she pastes into a booklet which, when full, can be redeemed for a twenty-five dollar Victory Bond.

When I walk to school, I see the flags with silver stars in many windows indicating that a person in that house is in the armed forces. I shudder with a pang of sorrow every time I pass a window with a gold star indicating that a person in that home has been killed in the war. Even an eleven-year old discovers the horrors of World War II.

GRANDPY FRIEBERGER'S GLADIOLAS

My grandfather and I are in business. "I depend on you, Morris," he says. "We own several hundred thousand gladiolas." No, I have never counted them, but I tell you that it takes weeks to plant them, placing the corms, or bulbs, cheek to jowl in a row. When spring arrives, Grandpy Freiberger, as I call him, finds that magic time after the rains have turned the rented fields into mud and before the longer days of sunshine bake the surface. He doesn't own power equipment, so he hires someone with a tractor to plow and harrow the soil.

Now it's time to plant. My grandpa fastens one end of the string to a stake at the far end of the field; I hold the other end as taut as I can. Then he sets out with a hand-powered machine called a wheel hoe with various attachments for cultivating the soil. Sometimes this contraption has blades to till the soil and kill weeds; now the attachment he is using makes a V-shaped ditch for planting. I watch his tall frame lean into the two oaken handles and make furrows four inches deep. No longer

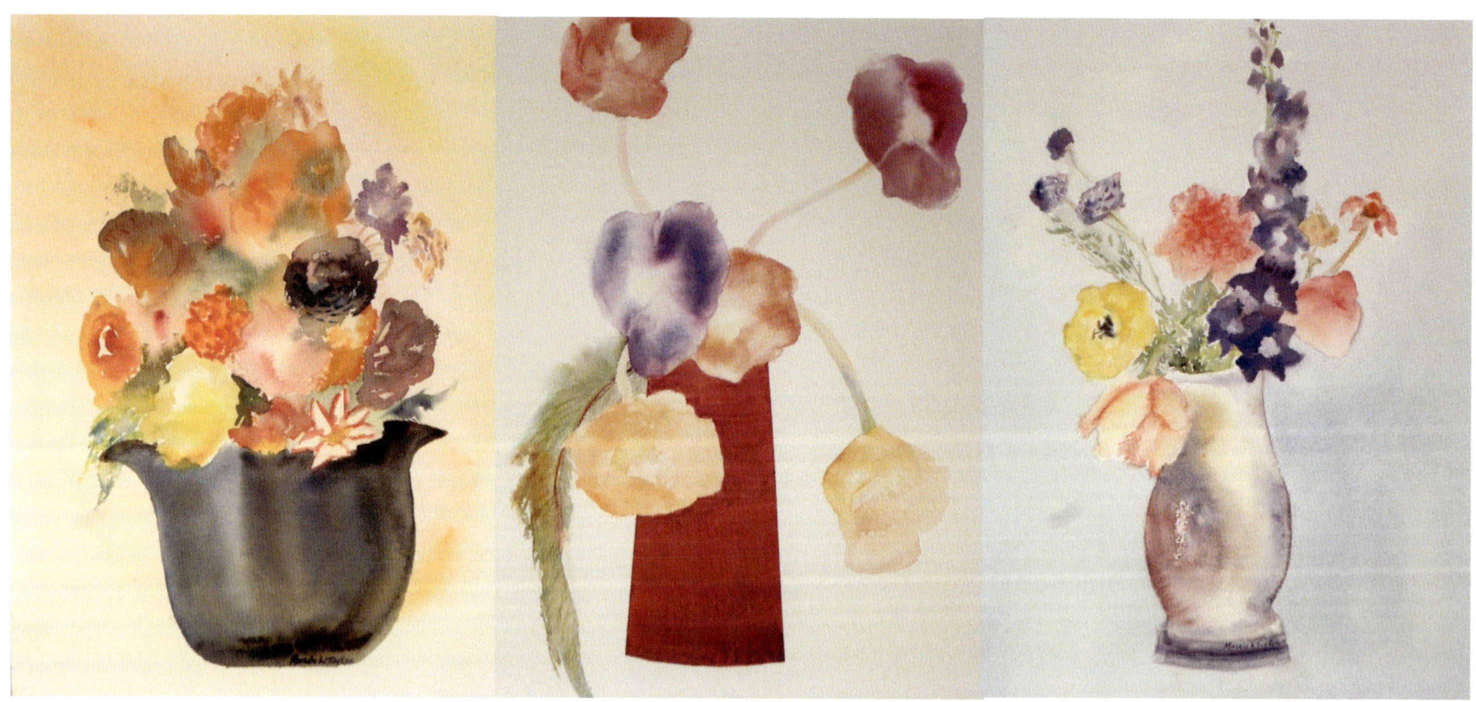

Bouquet Series: 16x12

does he need the string. He fixes his eye ahead and makes another straight row parallel and equidistant without the aid of a stretched line. I follow quickly spreading some manure we have hauled from the chicken houses. Grandpa mixes it with a hoe. Into those trenches I place the gladiola bulbs, shoulder-to-shoulder, bud side up. I am tall enough to help cover the corms.

"Be careful not to mix the lots," my grandfather warns. "No one wants to buy a mixture of colors these days." Each variety not only has different coloration patterns, but also differing growth habits. I faithfully place a stake bearing the technical name, such as the salmon colored Picardy or the lavender ruffled Elizabeth the Queen.

On sunny days Grandpy runs the wheel hoe. I do the weeding on my knees. My sixty-year-old grandfather says that I am closer to the ground than he is. Throughout the season, I enjoy watching the flowers grow, especially when the tall stems start to show color.

This particular Saturday night is like many others in late July and August. Usually Grandpy Freiberger and I pick gladiolas during the day. Flowers grow all day long on Saturday, but my grandpa and I are Seventh-day Adventists, and on that day we do not work in the fields.

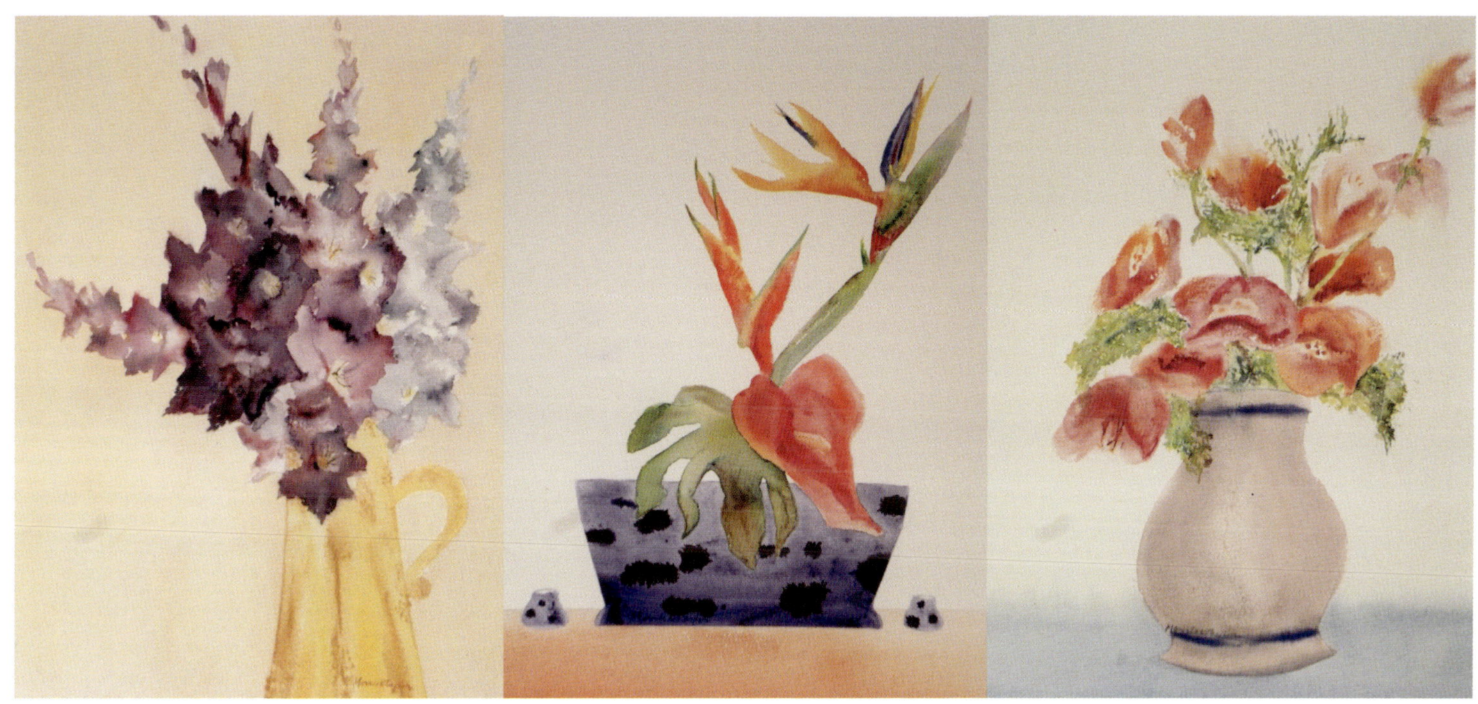

Bouquet Series: 16x12

We keep Sabbath like Jewish people from Friday sundown until the sun has set on Saturday. To get the gladiolas to market in the wee hours of Sunday, I help him pick in the late evening with the help of a kerosene lamp.

Grandpy's sharp knife deftly makes a cut downward, then a sharp turn upward to include several leaves on the stiff stalk. He adds them one by one to the heap of gladiolas accumulating in my outstretched arms. The pile reaches my nose.

"I can't hold any more," I say.

"Take them to the truck and put them carefully in the buckets of water." One of my arms has a big red ring where the bale of the kerosene lantern hangs. Both arms ache. "And don't mix the colors."

I love to be with my grandfather. My stepfather doesn't do things with me. Grandpa and I are a team, and I don't complain. Besides, he gives me a nickel extra above my usual ten cents an hour for working on Saturday night. I feel grown-up when Grandpy trusts me. Sometimes he takes me on the sales route to Worcester and then down the pike toward Boston. I like the Moreschi Florists, three brothers of Italian descent, because they answer my questions about plants. I think they call it *floriculture*.

I really enjoy the important trip to Mansfield, Massachusetts. There we visit the experimental fields where they develop new varieties of gladioli. "How come these blooms look so different," I ask.

Grandpa explains the process of cross-pollination. "Each one of the individual florets has the male part which makes the pollen; all these are removed. By hand the gardener germinates the pistol, the female part, with the pollen from another plant that has the characteristics he wants to breed."

"Is that why there are so many different kinds of gladiola?"

"Yes, endless possibilities. Look at these wonderful new varieties. Not only is the farmer seeking desirable colors, but growth characteristics as well, like those tall, straight ones over there."

"How come those rows looks so wilted?"

"The grower has to destroy those right away. They are diseased, the dreaded thrips infestation.

"Is that why we soak the bulbs in that stinky, high-powered disinfectant?"

"You're right, Morris. But the most important thing this farm does is developing new varieties. I'm hoping that I can afford some of the newly created pure white ones coveted for weddings. They cost a dollar for each bloom-sized bulb. My florist customers are willing to pay a premium price for the improved blooms, not just the fifteen to twenty-five cents per dozen that we get for the standard colors."

"How do you get more bulbs for next year?"

"When we dig them up next autumn, some of the bulbs will be larger, others will multiply into two or three bulbs. Clinging to each large group will be a cluster of six to a dozen smaller mini bulbs, or bulblets. The small ones will develop to blooming size in two or three seasons."

"That's hard work and a long time to wait. I'll be here to help you, Grandpa."

When my grandfather dies, I inherit thousands of his precious gladiola corms. Now I am business. I earn some of my graduate school expenses by growing and peddling the blooms. The last of them are refused entry into the State of California when I move there to teach at Pacific Union College above the Napa Valley. Sadly, I surrender them to the border inspectors for disposal. The corms are gone like burned out incandescent light bulbs, but the memory of those halcyon days with my grandfather and our gladiolas lingers.

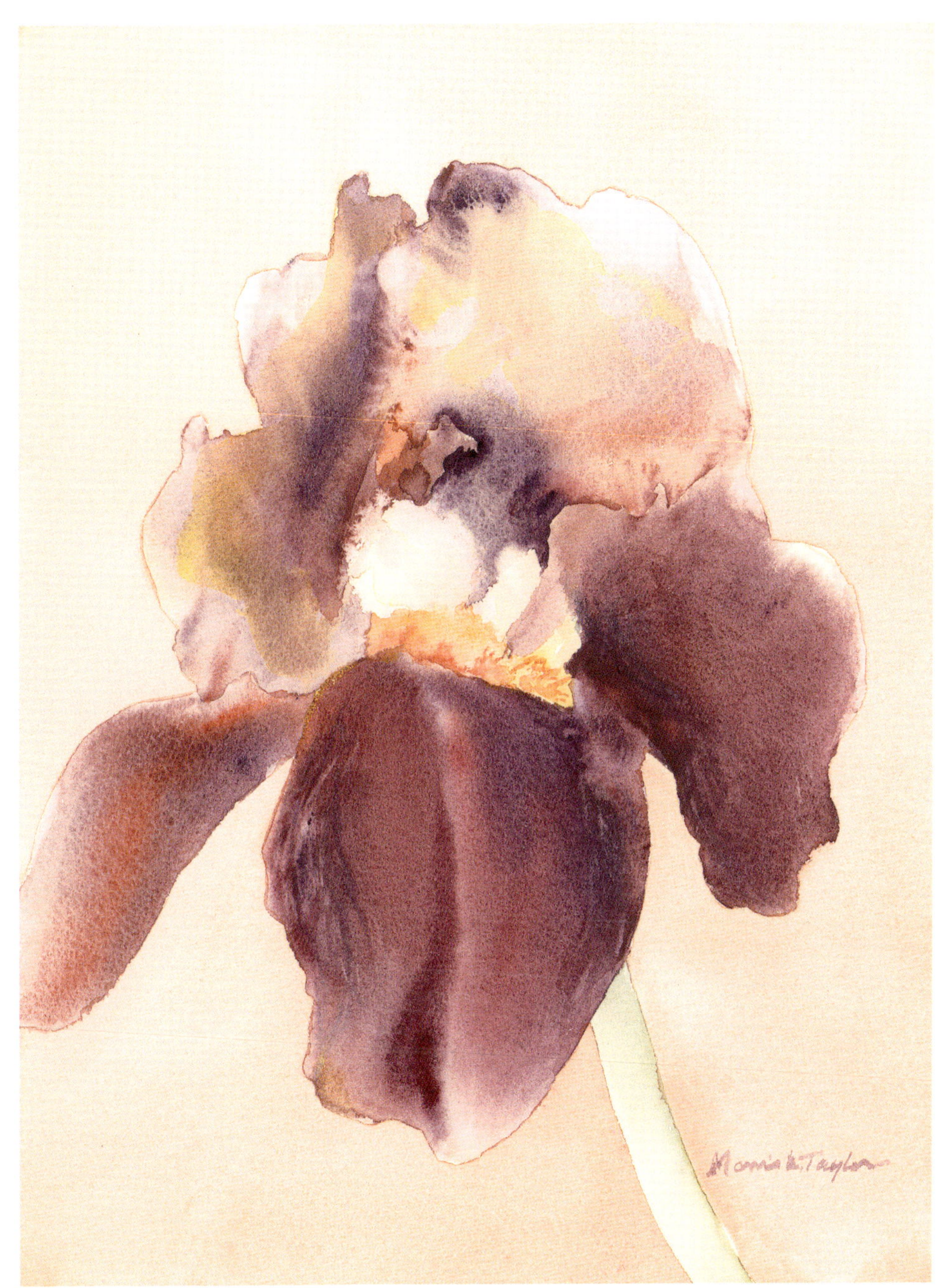

Multi-colored Iris, 12x9

Farming with a Horse

I am driving a rental car from Boston's Logan Airport to South Lancaster, Massachusetts, a prim town established in 1653. I look forward to revisiting the Lancaster town square. The library boasts a complete elephant portfolio of Audubon's birds and a banner welcoming General Lafayette in the Revolutionary War. Charles Bullfinch, who also designed the U. S. Capitol and the Massachusetts State House, drew the plans for the brick church. I am making the pilgrimage to Lancaster to celebrate the fiftieth anniversary of my graduation from Atlantic Union College in 1951.

Taking the ramp off the modern Interstate 260 onto local Route 62 in Berlin, I have to slow to a crawl. *Not another detour*, I say to myself. *I'm already kind of lost. Things don't look the same as I remember.*

Grudgingly I turn the wheel of my rental car to follow the orange signs. The terrain seems familiar. I slow down to enjoy the sights from my teen years. The typical New England stone fences delineate property boundaries. A brook gurgles over smooth stones. In a glint of sunbeam an iridescent dragonfly hovers over watercress waving in the gentle current.

"I've been here before," I exclaim aloud. "There's the Beckner Farm."

Perched on the hillside is the white clapboard manse. The shutters are still green, though faded and in need of repair. At the first opportunity, I turn onto the shoulder of the winding country road.

I open the car door. I savor the scent of evergreen resin, and my eyes blink from the sun reflecting upon the flame-colored maples. As my feet shuffle noisily in dry leaves, I think, *Ah, New England in the autumn! Is there anything more glorious?*

When I catch a glimpse of the waterfall, I feel a wave of nostalgia. In this sequestered spot the water drops from the stone and earth dam a dozen feet high in delicate rivulets and wider splashes. Here I used to shower on a hot summer day after working in the field, leading a horse while my grandfather held firmly to the cultivator. This cascading water feels shivery and brings goose bumps even in July. At home there was no running water, just a well with a rope to pull up the bucket.

I cross the street and wander toward the barn. Remembered fear makes me shudder. The huge structure needs a new roof just as it did six decades ago when I helped my grandfather put tarred paper on it with galvanized roofing nails. We would wait until the hottest July day to slather hot tar over the joints of the roofing paper. I still experience acrophobia thinking about that steep roof, the high eaves, and the sloping hillside below.

I am eager to confirm a childhood memory. There it is, a shed now needing props to keep the sagging building upright. The icehouse has thick double walls. The space between the upright studs and floor joists is filled with sawdust. In winter my grandpa helps the aging Mr. Beckner cut blocks of ice from the millpond. With horse and sleigh they haul them up to this shed. In summer my grandfather shows me how to open and close the door of the icehouse quickly. With iron tongs he grabs a block of ice, placing it on the back of the Model T pickup. He takes his ice pick and gives me a piece of ice to suck on as we drive the mile to our place on Mill Street Extension. In the entryway my parents have a large ice chest with a metal compartment big enough to hold a forty-pound chunk of ice, which lasts several days. On holidays like the Fourth of July, we make ice cream with some of this ice and rock salt in a hand-cranked freezer.

The Beckner family had a long friendship with my grandfather, James Freiberger, and his first wife, my grandmother, Frances. They studied together at the same school, Atlantic Union College, from which I graduated. The elder Beckner was ordained and became a missionary to North Africa. Upon his return he set up a feather duster factory for his retirement years. Ostrich feathers, imported from Africa, were popular. The finest and frilliest plumes were sold for ladies' millinery. The coarser ones were attached in circular rows onto sticks of varying lengths to become feather dusters. These came in handy for fancy folk who furnished their parlors with Edwardian knick-knacks.

The earliest recollection that I have of the Beckner farm is faint, but I know the memory is mine, because no adult has ever spoken of it in my presence. Old lady Beckner, as my kin called her, was frail. To a young boy she looks like an apparition with her lacy nightcap and knitted bed jacket. The room is dark. People speak in whispers. As I now look up at the house, I cannot recall which room was hers. I know it was on the second floor because a carved staircase with a banister and carpeted risers captured my boyish imagination. *These people are rich*, my young child's mind thought.

My grandfather was ordained as a Seventh-day Adventist preacher just like his classmate, George Beckner; however, my grandpa, Elder James Freiberger, was laid off from the Southern New England Conference payroll during the arrival of the Great Depression, so his life took a different course. But the friendship of these two men made it possible for my family to rent some land on this ancestral farm to raise sweet corn, potatoes and other truck garden vegetables to subsist.

This day I remember that the only photo I possess of grandfather and me together shows him with his stiff hands and bony body leaning against the wood and iron cultivator and me with my lanky body gingerly holding the bridle of the huge workhorse. I remember the dusty furrows, the salty sweat and tired muscles. In my mind the stings of horse flies still burn and the blisters still ooze.

MUSIC OR MEDICINE?

I, a seventeen-year-old college sophomore, obsess about this decision, music or medicine. Frequently at religious gatherings and social occasions I play the piano. My friends assume that music is to be my career. During my parochial high school and fundamentalist college years, I ace classes in both music and medicine. In my adolescent mind I sense the prestige attached to the medical professions and realize that I can compete. I also desire to serve in the forefront of those serving the world's needs, probably as a missionary physician. Yet, I love music. Can I earn a living playing the piano and teaching music, particularly since I had no lessons until I was in the eighth grade?

Adventists hold their annual camp meeting during the week of Independence Day. In the industrial towns of Massachusetts, Connecticut and Rhode Island, factories often shut down during the week of July 4, and workers take their vacation at that time. Faithful Seventh-day Adventist families spend all ten days at the encampment. On weekends the ranks of worshippers swell by more casual visitors and by breadwinners who cannot spare the days from work.

Faithful Adventists are already arriving at the campgrounds. I smell the vast field of new mown grass. Frequent thundershowers turn the walkways into slippery mud. When the sun comes out, the rows of tan tents reflect the sunlight at rakish angles. The thin walls hold no secrets. In larger meeting tents children sing their hearts out, listen to character building stories and work out their mischief. The huge meeting tent seating a thousand people has been replaced by a wooden tabernacle with a low slung, black-tarred roof.

For me this summer is extra busy. Each weekday morning I walk the three-mile circuit for a 7:30 a.m. science class that will apply toward pre-med. I hike between the neighboring towns of South Lancaster and Clinton. I eat my lunch en route. At the commercial laundry in Clinton I sort dirty clothes to earn tuition. The third leg of the triangle leads me back home. My class notecards are always with me; I even prop them at my workbench. Only when I practice the piano do I find release from the grinding routine.

One summer evening my mother is lying in bed crocheting baby booties. Each pair has a place for the insertion of a pink or blue ribbon if you know the sex of the baby, green or yellow if in doubt. I ask her what she thinks about my educational dilemma. Her answer comes swiftly. "You can do whatever you want. You're the one who has to earn it."

I know that already. I ask my teachers and classmates. They say, "A talented guy like you should be a gospel preacher or a medical doctor."

When I express a tendency toward music, the dismissive response is often, "That's nice."

The choice of profession becomes existential. I believe that if I am devout enough, the Good Lord will answer me in some concrete way at a time of His choosing. The camp meeting is my opportunity. I voraciously devour all the spiritual books available. I look over the volumes for sale at the book tent. None meet my interest or my budget. During the announcement time at the Thursday evening meeting, ushers walk up and down the aisle hawking the religious book of the evening. The first fifty persons who put their hand up may buy the paperback for fifty cents. That's the lunch money I have in my pocket, and I squander the four bits for this prized possession.

Immediately I embark upon reading "Fundamentals of Christian Education," by the Adventist writer, Ellen G. White. My religion teaches me that she is the church prophet on an equal footing with Biblical seers of old. Each day my private devotions consist of reading a chapter followed by earnest prayer.

One particular evening I am so bone tired that I pull the covers up around my neck and almost fall asleep. Then I remember my pledge. Sitting bolt upright, I finger the red paper cover. The bookmark has fallen out, so I nonchalantly turn the pages. I determine to read that random chapter to the end. Toward the close I wearily mouth the words, "It is not necessary for so many young men to study medicine." Without question I believe this to be the providential answer. I immediately fall asleep.

The next morning these words are the first thing I think about. I am happy and relieved. School and work have new focus.

When I return home about suppertime, my mother meets me at the door. "What have you done, Morris?"

"Nothing special."

"You must have done something! Here's a letter from the president."

I take the letter to my tiny sleeping room on the porch. I nervously open the envelope. I notice that it is imprinted, Office of the President, Atlantic Union College. I read aloud, "In appreciation for your artistic service to A. U. C., you are awarded a full scholarship for your piano lessons, Dr. L. N. Holmes." No such scholarship exists; it has been created out of the blue just for me. I know: *Music is my profession and life work.*

Now as an octogenarian, I look back on a fulfilled career as a classical concert pianist and teacher. I am a Professor Emeritus of Music. My belief trajectory has taken me away from a literal view of prophecy; however, I am grateful for that teenage vision of what I could become.

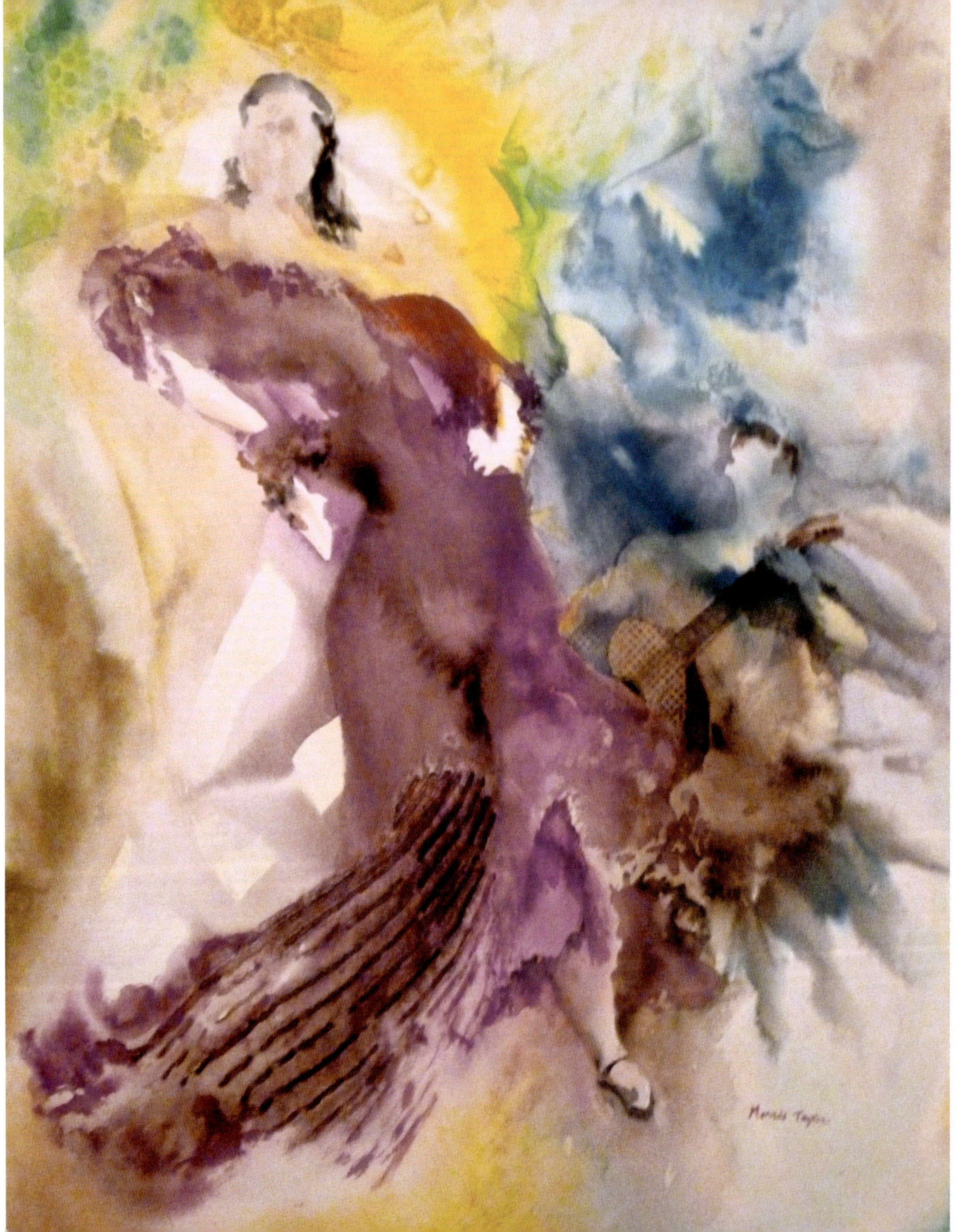

Flamenco Dancer,
29x22

SWEET ON THE SAME GIRL

In 1952, I meet Herbert Blomstedt in Boston. I am a freshman teacher at my alma mater and also a full time graduate student at Boston University. Herbert is in Boston on the Swedish equivalent of a Fulbright Scholar. His erect frame exudes confidence. Immediately I am intrigued by his uncanny concentration. Herbert's intelligent manor of conducting an orchestra shows him to be a consummate artist who is serious about authentic music performances.

Emerging from Symphony Subway Station, Herbert and I walk catty-corner from Symphony Hall to the New England Conservatory of Music. As we saunter into the rear of Jordan Concert Hall, the student orchestra is rehearsing. Hardly have we seated ourselves in the near empty auditorium when the conductor senses Herbert's presence.

"Come here." The conductor beckons. "I want to see what the balance sounds like in various parts of the hall."

Herbert strides to the podium. Closing the musical score, he announces, "We will begin at letter H," a specific location for rehearsal purposes. From memory he conducts the near professional student orchestra to the completion of the third movement of Beethoven's *Sixth Symphony*.

A few months later I travel by bus to New York City. Herbert has invited me to stay with him in his sublet room near Riverside Cathedral. I sleep on the couch springs, and he lies on the thin cushions that are moved to the floor.

His clothes hang to dry in the miniature bathroom.

Early in the morning I hear the rustling of music pages. "Good morning, Morris. Do you know this work? I'm memorizing it for Lenny this week."

My eyes are partially stuck shut; I make out the principal melody of a major symphony. "I'm quite sure I have heard this piece. Sounds Scandinavian; maybe Sibelius."

"Pretty close. Nielsen is neglected these days."

"Did you say you were coaching with Leonard Bernstein?"

"Yes, I go to his studio on the upper East side of Central Park. I memorize a major orchestral score every week preparing for his tutelage."

While eating an improvised breakfast prepared on a hot plate, I ask, "Do you know of any exciting concerts in town?"

"There's a chamber music program at Town Hall tonight, the Budapest String Quartet. I think Serkin is joining them for the Brahms *Piano Quintet*. I have a pair of tickets in the balcony for you and me."

"I love chamber music. Thanks for the offer, but I can't really accept. I plan on taking Elaine out tonight," I say.

"You mean Elaine Myers?"

"Oh! Didn't I tell you that she and I are getting acquainted? She's here working on her Master's degree at Columbia Teacher's College."

"Here, take the pair of tickets. Enjoy!"

That evening, Elaine and I are hardly settled into our balcony seats, when Herbert taps me on the shoulder.

"How did you get in? I thought that …" I say.

"Never mind. I've got my ways," says Herbert. "See you at intermission."

In our hallway conversation I discover that Herbert bought those tickets for Elaine and himself. They are becoming good friends. Elaine accompanies Herbert on the pipe organ while he plays the violin for church. I envy Herbert for his advantage of living in the same city as Elaine while I am teaching at Atlantic Union College two hundred miles to the north, and me without a car or money.

The next day Herbert plans an adventure. Elaine is not available. She has a cameo appearance at the Faith for Today television program, where she works as a secretary grading "It is Written" viewer answer sheets. The only clue I have about Herbert's plan is the fact that Toscanini will be rehearsing for a concert with the NBC Orchestra.

About nine the next morning Herbert commands, "Grab your coat. We're walking to Carnegie Hall."

"But Hebert, I really don't have enough cash."

"Don't worry. I'm taking care of it," says Herbert.

As we approach the venerable performing venue for musicians, I am excited. "Herbert, I don't think the ticket office is open," I say.

"You're right. Arturo Toscanini never allows anyone into his rehearsals. Just follow me"

The huge stage door rises forbiddingly before the two of us. A tall guy, the height of a basketball star, tries to solicit money from us in exchange for some pornographic pics. Herbert hands him several bills but explains, "I don't want your porn. I need you to open that door."

To my amazement the man stands on tiptoe and reaches to the top. His strong fingers release the locking mechanism. The doors crack open just enough to allow us to slip through. In the style of burglars, Herbert and I sneak up the stairs into one of the second tier boxes. I can smell the dusty drapes as we hold them open a crack. Through the gilded grating we peer at the historic moment transpiring on the stage below.

All members of the NBC Symphony rise. From stage left Toscanini totters to the podium. Then he straightens his hunched back and transforms himself into a ferocious maestro. Toscanini projects a perfectionist precision even in his mid eighties. One emerging conductor named Herbert and one freshman piano professor named Morris are duly awestruck by Toscanini's consummate musicianship.

In the summer of 1953 I travel to the Tanglewood Music Center, the gathering place for classical musicians in the Berkshire Mountains of Western Massachusetts. On Sunday Herbert Blomstedt will compete for the Koussevitsky prize. By dint of his brilliance, Herbert has joined Leonard Bernstein's coterie of three private students. Risking his chance at the coveted Koussevitsky prize, Herbert has declined to rehearse the Boston Symphony Orchestra on the Sabbath Day. Both Herbert and I are members of the Seventh-day Adventist Church and observe Sabbath from sundown on Friday to sunset on Saturday. Although Herbert has a lifelong commitment not to rehearse on the Sabbath, which is work, he can, however, choose to *perform* great music on the Sabbath, which is for the ethical good of humanity.

Over the years Herbert and I have kept a meaningful, yet distant friendship. I develop as Professor of Music and decent concert pianist. He becomes a renowned conductor with an international reputation. He wins the Koussevitsky prize in orchestral conducting. I capture the other prize. Elaine and I are married in 1955.

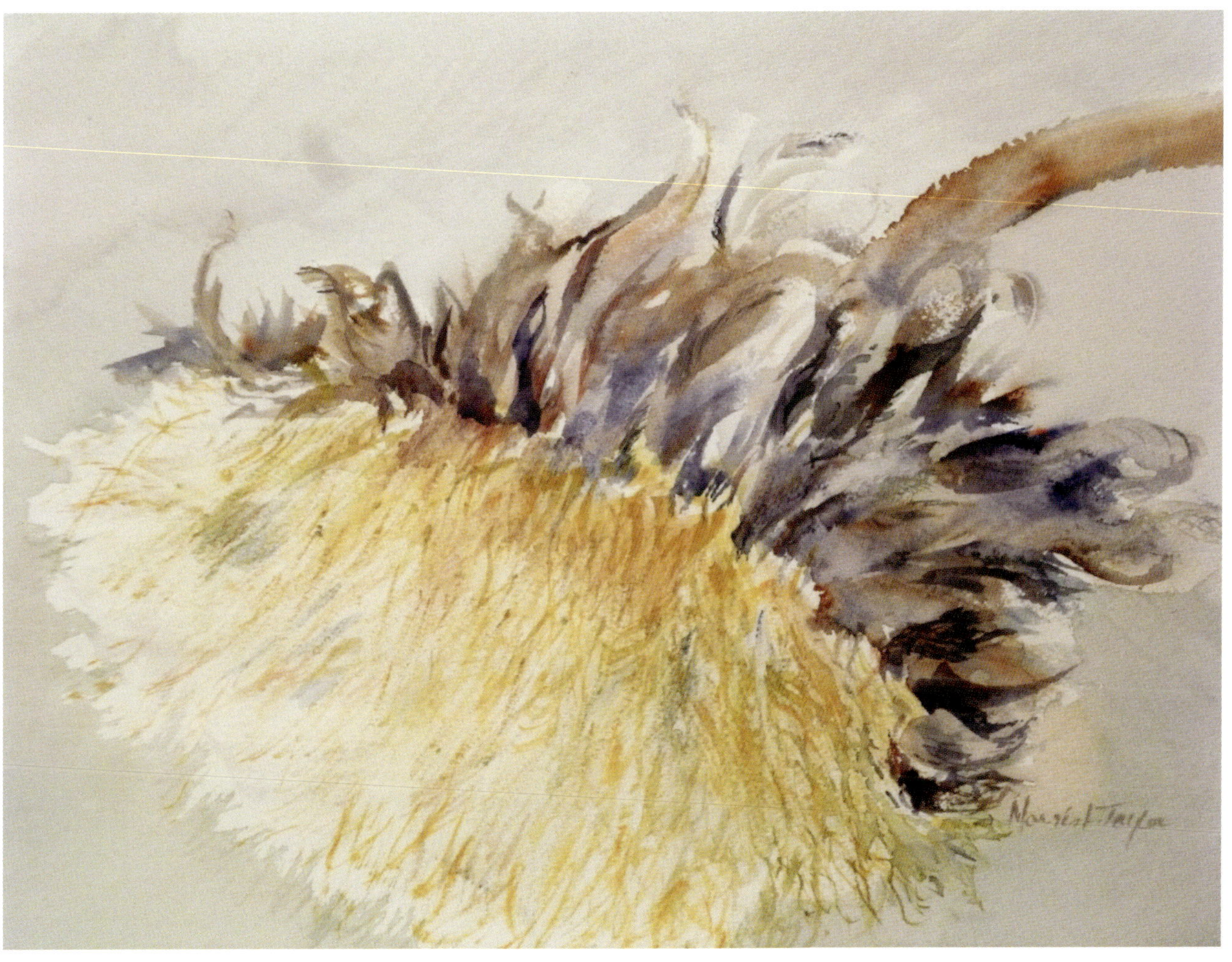

Drying Thistle   12x9

ARMY EXPERIENCES

I nervously rip open a letter from the local draft board. "Your fellow citizens require you to report for duty in the United States Army on December 7, 1953."

The next day I knock on the door of my friend, Dr. George Shankel, the academic dean of Atlantic Union College. "Sir, I am sad to tell you," I say, "that I cannot continue my teaching. Yesterday I just received my draft papers to report thirty days from now."

"That's strange," Dr. Shankel replies. "I thought that full time faculty members were exempt."

"Yes, I did too. In addition to my professorship, I am concurrently enrolled as a full time doctoral student at Boston University," I continue somewhat out of breath. "That should also gain me an exemption from service in the military."

"Do you think that you will see active duty after the basic training?" the dean asks.

"There is no guarantee," I reply. "At least I will not have to kill anyone. When I registered with the government at age eighteen, I also explained why I am a conscientious objector. I am willing to serve my country, but not bear arms."

Dean Shankel scowls as he reads the draft notice. His deep set eyes regain their usual twinkle as he says, "Well, Morris, there is nothing you nor I can do but comply. I'll miss you. You're an effective professor, and your students like you. Your job will be waiting for you when you come back in two years."

"What do you think will become of me; will I be the same or different?" I ask. "I've never really travelled outside of New England or New York State. I guess I've lived a rather sheltered life in parochial schools and among church conservatives."

"You'll see a slice of the world you did not know existed," he replies. "You have accomplished a lot in your twenty-two years. It's up to you how army life affects you. Some recruits turn their backs on their previous life and others return with maturity."

"Friends tell me that the army will put muscle on skinny guys like me," I joke to hide my fear. "At least I'm not married with a family to support like many draftees my age."

A month later, Dr. Shankel drives me to the induction center in Leominster, Massachusetts. A strong wind whips at my one-hundred-twenty-pound frame. Since my few instructions inform me that my personal possessions will be thrown away, I carry only a papier-mâché suitcase with flimsy clothes and toiletries. The troop train affords few amenities. I'm glad for the lunch I've brought.

Upon arrival at Fort Dix, New Jersey, I follow the rest of the recruits into a holding center. There we receive minimal bedding and a folding cot. After a few hours of fitful sleep, reveille awakens me at four a.m. I join the line at the mess hall. Moist breath confirms that the temperature has dipped below freezing. My civvies do not prevent the drifting snow from temporarily thawing, then forming icy patterns on my clothing.

When the sergeant calls for volunteers for an unspecified duty, I'm freezing cold and say, "Count me in."

I learn fast the first rule of army life: Don't volunteer, ever. I serve bacon for two and a half hours to the endless line of soldiers in the mess hall. I am a lifelong vegetarian. I certainly avoid any hog products, since even the smell makes me ill. When it is my turn to eat some food, I nearly throw up. An hour later at the welcoming ceremony the commanding officer tries to get a laugh, "Recruits, the hall is not called a 'Mess Hall' because the hall's a mess. It's because the food's a mess."

Fort Dix, as it turns out, is a welcoming center and transfer point. Within the week I am shipped to Camp Pickett, Virginia, for two months of basic training. Because I am a conscientious objector, I do not train with guns. When the other soldiers go to the firing range for weapons practice, I invariably get Kitchen Police duty. This means that I begin preparing breakfast at 4 a.m. and get off duty about 7 or 8 p.m., after all the dishes are clean, the floor mopped and the tables are set for morning. If there is a minor screw up on the range, KP is considered adequate punishment for delinquent soldiers. I draw KP duty most days because I do not train with weapons.

Before the evening meal the mail is distributed to the men of our company. I almost never get anything in the post, so I pay little attention. One day, about a month after I am inducted, when distributing mail the company sergeant barks, "Who's this Taylor guy?"

I cringe. My lips will not move. All I could do is raise my hand.

As I walk forward to receive a package, the abuse continues, "There are only flunky privates in Company A. No one here is a 'Private First Class.' Is that clear?"

Through my chagrin and embarrassment I read the label, "From Elaine Myers, To: Private First Class Morris Taylor." I take the parcel to my barracks and open it in private after the room is dark. I invite a buddy that I particularly like, named Lionel, to share some goodies: homemade cookies, carefully packed but broken in pieces; packets of nuts, roasted and salted; and healthful candy, fashioned from dried fruits and rolled in shredded cocoanut.

"Who's this Elaine?" Lionel asks.

"She's the one I was telling you about meeting in New York City. Elaine and that orchestra conductor, Blomstedt, were dating," I say.

"I thought that you told me that you weren't particularly interested in her. You said seven years older than you."

"Yes, Lionel, I did say that. Elaine has a chiseled face with prematurely white hair. Her erect posture and ballet figure make her look young. She has a great smile though and a sterling reputation. She's fun to be around when you need someone."

"But I don't think you are really attracted to her, are you? Like being really excited when you are having sex?" he observes.

"That's getting too close for comfort. I'm a virgin. My religion teaches me that pre-marital sex is evil. Anyway, it's just that someone cares about me."

I write Elaine a thank you note that needs an answer. This begins a correspondence that continues for a year and half. Sometimes the letters are general, at other times personal, but always welcome.

Other than this, life at Camp Picket is monotonous. I am eager to complete the mandatory basic training. Near the end of the eight weeks each soldier is required to go through one hellish maneuver. Under the fire of bullets, a rookie crawls on the ground through an obstacle course consisting of barbed wire, booby traps, smoke bombs and rough terrain.

The day arrives for our company to prove our bravery. The rain of the previous night has turned the course into an ochre and red ooze of mud. Wet clothing reveals the outlines of attractive bodies beneath.

"Keep your asses down!" barks the drill sergeant.

"Yes, Sir," come the obligatory shouts.

I cannot tell whether my shivering is from numbing fear or wet clothing.

Over the loud speaker I hear, "That was only a test run with blanks. The real bullets will fly this time around."

Wouldn't you think once was enough? I don't think I'll make it through twice. I'm physically exhausted. An inner drive calls up all the strength I can muster. No, you're not going to chicken out.

I crawl and climb to the end of the challenging course. As the sun comes out and dries my clothes and dry mud cakes my boots and hair, I lean against a fencepost in a seated position. I am studying a list of German vocabulary words that I carry in my pocket in preparation for an eventual return to completing my doctorate at Boston University. This music performance degree requires a reading knowledge of two languages.

"What you doing there, soldier?" comes a query from an unexpected voice.

"Just studying for my doctorate," I reply.

When I glance up, I see the silver bars. As I try desperately to scramble to my feet to salute properly, the Lieutenant in charge says, "At ease, soldier. As you were."

We exchange smiles. The officer ambles on, and I slump back to my comfortable position.

"*Whew! One court martial averted*," I gasp silently. I should have saluted the highest ranking officer in my battalion. *Maybe he is also a college man*, I muse.

I pass this exercise in overcoming fear of combat and the other requirements for my basic training at Camp Pickett in Virginia. In a few days my transfer papers arrive. One doesn't get a choice about assignments in the army. Two days later I board a khaki-painted bus. I discover that the unknown destination is an army airfield. As I step up the rickety stairs leading into the hold of a troop plane, I struggle with a duffle bag carrying all my mortal possessions. There are no windows on the plane. I copy my buddies as they line their duffle bags up along the wall and sit on them. With a shiver and shake the plane takes off. My heart races; my fingertips blanch; and my nails dig into my thighs. This is my first plane ride. I feel kidnapped.

When I arrive, I discover that I am at Fort Sam Houston in San Antonio, Texas. Since I am a conscientious objector, I assume that I am about to be assigned to the medical corp. I hear a rumor that at this time, Fort Sam Houston, so-called "Home of the Army Medic," only serves as a center for troop transfer.

I am waiting at the mess hall with all my gear. One of the cutest guys in the line asks me, "Hey, buddy. Where are you from?"

I answer shyly, "Boston."

"Oh," he mocks with a twang, "you're one of the those Tea Party boys!"

"Yeah," I retort in a broad accent. "I pak my ca by the Chales Rivah."

I wish I could get to know this handsome smarty-pants better, but the stay in San Antonio is short. Within the week my orders arrive. They require me to report to Fort Hood, Texas, the largest military post, home of the First Armored Division, also known as "Hell on Wheels." I am issued a bus ticket with orders to report for duty the next day at the army base outside Killeen, Texas. I am bitterly disappointed. I have volunteered to go overseas, hoping for a military assignment in Germany or some other place in Europe. Still, I suppose Texas is better than being assigned to Korea where the shooting war is just subsiding.

No use to report early, I think. How wrong can I be? When I get the army base, the first words I hear are, "Go to the commissary and pick up your supplies." Down at the commissary, I grab a wool blanket, mess gear and a shelter half to match with a buddy's other half to make sleeping accommodations for two. "Jump onto the back of that two-and-a-half-ton truck," commands the sergeant on duty. I obey and off I go to an undisclosed location.

Now here I am in the middle of nowhere. I think to myself. Make the best of the situation. Am I am the only one ejected into the darkness of midnight? "I throw the half tent I was issued over a grassy knoll and clothe myself in all the warm things I can find.

I feel alone. No pictures of a sweetheart left behind.

My mother and a nearly illiterate stepfather do not write. Elaine is the only person who corresponds with me regularly, but she doesn't know where I am newly stationed.

I dream of hot men, but I am smart enough to suppress my homosexuality. I imagine that in the surrounding chaparral there may be many men my age. In my subconscious mind I realize that I would not dare not make any sexual advances that would ruin my army career and jeopardize my potential as a professor in a church-related university.

The smell of food awakens me. I'm cold and starved. I put on my boots, grab the mess kit and follow my nose to the makeshift field kitchen. I discover that I am not alone. There is an encampment about a couple of hundred yards over the next hill. I fall in line. No one asks for ID. One attractive recruit reaches with tongs into the hot water of a garbage can heated over an open fire. "Take this one," he repeats frequently as he fishes out a drab-colored tin. "You don't have a choice, soldier," he says to me. "Grab one of those packets, stupid. Can't you see the coffee's over there?"

Returning to my secluded spot, I open the C-ration. I'd rather not think about what is in the mish-mash hash. I just wolf it down. I open the accompanying packet—toilet paper, toothbrush and paste, and matches. I enjoy the circular cracker covered with chocolate that was included in the packet.

The next day must be Sunday. Through the dark green leaves of the live oak and the more colorful and oily leaves of poison oak I can see men gathering around a table and pulpit. I saunter over to the natural amphitheater and sit on the ground like everyone else.

"Anybody here play the organ?"

I raise my hand and head toward the portable instrument. I am familiar with my step-great-grandmother's pump organ, so I feel right at home. The chaplain hands me a hymnbook. I manage to prop the pages open against the morning breeze.

After a week of not knowing why I am living in the chaparral, I realize that I probably was the only recruit to arrive that day after the assignments for the maneuvers have been made. I return by truck to the center of the post. Only then do I receive my orders to become a Chaplain's Assistant.

There are three chaplains in our office and three assistants who serve them. I enjoy the friendship of a slim, gregarious guy named Curt; but I respond to his sexual overtures with indifference to avoid getting involved or caught. A muscular, jolly guy named Peter is the chaplain's assistant who works with the Roman Catholic priest, Chaplain McGoohan. I don't get to know Peter very well. On weekends he spends his off-duty hours in the single officer's quarters with various men of rank.

On weekdays I type letters, clean the latrine, maintain the Jeep, make the coffee, and attend to anything else that needs doing. On Sunday I play the Hammond organ at the post chapel for three services, each church service requiring a different aesthetic. The Episcopal chaplain

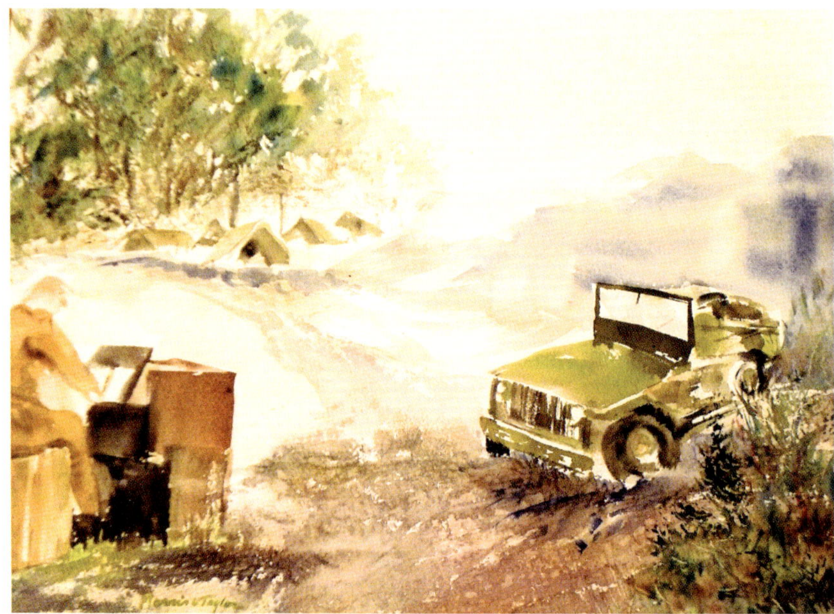

Fort Hood Bivouac, 12x16

prefers more formal church music. Evangelical types enjoy gospel music. The Roman Catholic service is mostly meditation before and after the Mass.

Several letters a week from Elaine make the army palatable. Working in the Chaplain's office gives me access to a typewriter making it easier to answer her letter the same day as it arrives. Most of the time both she and I use these written exchanges for keeping in touch about events and getting acquainted. Gradually, the sharing becomes more intimate. Maybe she thinks I am courting her; I tell myself to take care and not become too involved romantically.

For good behavior and quality service on six days, Chaplain Hopson, the Southern Baptist chaplain for whom I work directly, approves my request to leave Fort Hood to attend church on Saturday. My company commander and the charge sergeant issue the coveted pass. On Saturday morning, relishing the freedom, but with almost no money in my pocket, I decide to hitchhike to Waco, Texas, where I hear there is a Seventh-day Adventist church. I dress in my civilian attire for the first time in many months.

I arrive on the doorstep of the Seventh-day Adventist Church before anyone else. The first persons there have no key, so we introduce ourselves and chat.

"We're the Faudis; Erma and John. We live north of here on a farm."

"Hi, I'm Morris, a chaplain's assistant from the army base about sixty miles south of here."

"Oh, I thought you were the new pastor," says Erma. "We're expecting him today."

"Haven't you met him or his family yet?" I ask.

John replies, "No, we haven't. Rumor has it that he's an older man who is single. I thought you might be Pastor Thomas."

"Isn't that a bit odd," I counter. Secretly I wonder what that signifies.

The conversation turns to Waco as home of the Branch Davidians, an offshoot of the Seventh-day Adventist Church. "You're not one of those radical people up the road, are you?" asks Erma, referring to the sect known for their weird notions of end-of-time prophecy and their eagerness for Armageddon.

"No, I'm not. In fact, I know little about them," I say to allay their fears. Evidently their incendiary behavior has split the local church and inflamed the national organization as well.

Other people arrive on the church doorstep. A deacon saunters up to the door and turns the key.

"Come on in. I apologize for being late. I was waiting for the new pastor to meet me at my house. I guess he's a "no show.""

"What will we do for the sermon?" a parishioner asks.

"Maybe this kind man will oblige us," says another man, looking like he has more authority. He addresses me plainly, "Will you preach the sermon?"

"Give me some time to think about it. I'll give you an answer in fifteen minutes," I reply. My answer is 'yes.' I preach an impromptu sermon on the story of Jesus about the parable of the talents to the accompaniment of audible amens.

The next Sabbath I again enter the modest church. Everyone looks around for the pianist to play the hymns for the meeting. From the platform the leader pleads, "Anyone here play the piano? It seems that Sister Maude is ill today."

What's a poor musician to do? Sit on his hands and live with his conscience? I volunteer. Everyone seems pleased with my style of piano playing. The congregation elects me as church pianist, choir director and Sabbath School teacher. The new preacher arrives that week. He is single. I wonder if he is a homosexual, like I secretly am.

After sundown I stand by the side of the main highway between Waco and Austin to hitchhike the sixty miles back to Fort Hood. An attractive guy with tight clothing and bulging muscles pulls to the curb and asks, "Hey, where you headed?"

"To Fort Hood near Killeen," I say.

"Jump in," the driver urges. "I am headed south. It's not much out of my way to take you to the army base."

"Sounds good to me," I say as I jump into the passenger seat.

Hardly have we pulled away from the curb when the driver's hand wanders onto my thigh. I'm excited sexually and scared emotionally. "No thanks," I say. "I just need a ride to Belton. That's on your route to Austin and won't take you out of your way."

"No one is expecting you tonight, are they?" the young guy asserts with some authority. "I'm planning on getting a hotel. You can stay with me."

"Yes, I have to report for duty at ten this evening," I counter, making up a lie as I go along. The driver seems angry and drives in an erratic manner.

"Trust me," the guy says. "I'll see that you get what you need and more."

As I try to keep a calm conversation going, I spy an unexpected red light across all lanes. I wait until the exact moment when I think the light is about to turn green; then I fling the door open and bolt across three lines of traffic to the curb. Horns honk. The driver has to proceed. I make my escape.

I determine to eschew gay men and return to the culture, the church and the college I know. I cannot risk being excoriated, excommunicated and expelled from everything I believe and live.

With no other mode of transportation, I crank up my courage to put my right thumb out to beg for another ride. Before ten that evening I am safely back at barracks. On my bed is a package from Elaine. During my wild ride I have worked up an appetite. I eagerly eat some roasted nuts and dried fruit from the box, the only food available at that hour the night.

Then I notice the hand-written envelope that was pasted to the front of the cardboard wrapping. Elaine wrote, "I'm inviting you to come visit me at my parents home in Portland, Oregon. I really want to become better acquainted with you in person. Spring break from my teaching at Walla Walla College comes this year from April 1-11, 1955. Can you arrange your army furlough at that time? My family is eager to meet you. Just maybe you can join the faculty at my college instead of returning to your alma mater back East."

That spring I make that trip by train. On the top of Mt. Tabor, near her parents' house in Southeastern Portland, I propose marriage. Elaine accepts. Two days later Elaine and I enjoy an engagement party quickly arranged by her family. I give Elaine her first orchid.

Her brother, Don Myers, lingers to have a confidential talk with me. "Did you know that the only man to whom my sister has been previously engaged turned out to be gay?" Don says. "I don't want that to happen again."

"Don," I reply, "I'll take good care of Elaine. I promise to satisfy all her needs. We plan to raise a family just like you and your wife, Dorothy."

After two years of military service, I am honorably

discharged. My chaplain, Lt Colonel Brannon J. Hopson, writes, "You have demonstrated your ability to adapt yourself to the hardships and rigors of military life with willingness and enthusiasm … Throughout you have maintained the highest integrity."

I marry Elaine at the Sunnyside Church on Labor Day of 1955. The ceremony is traditional. Elaine sews her own wedding dress from a Vogue pattern, a ballerina length gown in off-white with a pink under-petticoat. I insist on gladiolas in memory of my grandfather's raising thousands of these bulbs. The music is totally composed by our friends for the entire ceremony including the organ music, choir anthems and chamber music.

I ask my brother, Skippy, "How can we escape our mischief makers? Some of the teenage rowdies want to hide our clothes, disable our get-away car and other tricks."

"Don't worry," says Skippy. "I've got everything under control. I can't tell you the details. Just follow me after the reception."

"Okay," I agree. "I have no other choice. Don't let me down."

After the wedding Elaine and I hop into the borrowed car and make chase with tin cans rattling. "Where are our suitcases?" Elaine asks. "Your brother, Don, assures me that he put them in the trunk of our car when no one else was around. I have to trust him."

Suddenly there is a lurch as I apply the brakes. Skippy points out the car window and yells, "Your car is on the other side of that guard rail." I pull up beside the continuous fence of the thruway. "I'll help you over. Your car is parked right there," he says. "Don locked your belongings in the trunk."

Sure enough, Don emerges from our car. "Yup, everything's there ready for the drive to the cottage you rented. Here are your keys. Now give me mine."

Elaine and I honeymoon at Zigzag on the slopes of Mount Hood. The murmurs of the adjacent river soothe our jitters. We cuddle to keep warm from the chill of the higher elevation. Soon the fireplace warms the center of the cozy cabin. Gradually Elaine becomes comfortable being alone with me and I with her. When we finally climb into bed with each other for the first time, we consummate our marriage. The bloody emission proves my wife is as virgin. And so am I. Both Elaine and I want to have several children. We keep our marriage vows absolutely until death does us part.

I join the faculty of Walla Walla College, a Seventh-day Adventist institution where Elaine is an Associate Professor of Music, teaching voice and choir. Because of vocal chord nodules, Elaine changes her performance area from voice to piano. Elaine and I become duo-pianists who concertize extensively. After my eight years as Chairman of the Division of Fine Arts at Southern Missionary College, in Tennessee, the Taylors move to Berrien Springs, where Elaine and I become tenured faculty members of the music department at Andrews University in Southwestern Michigan. As our four children mature musically, they join the musical troupe.

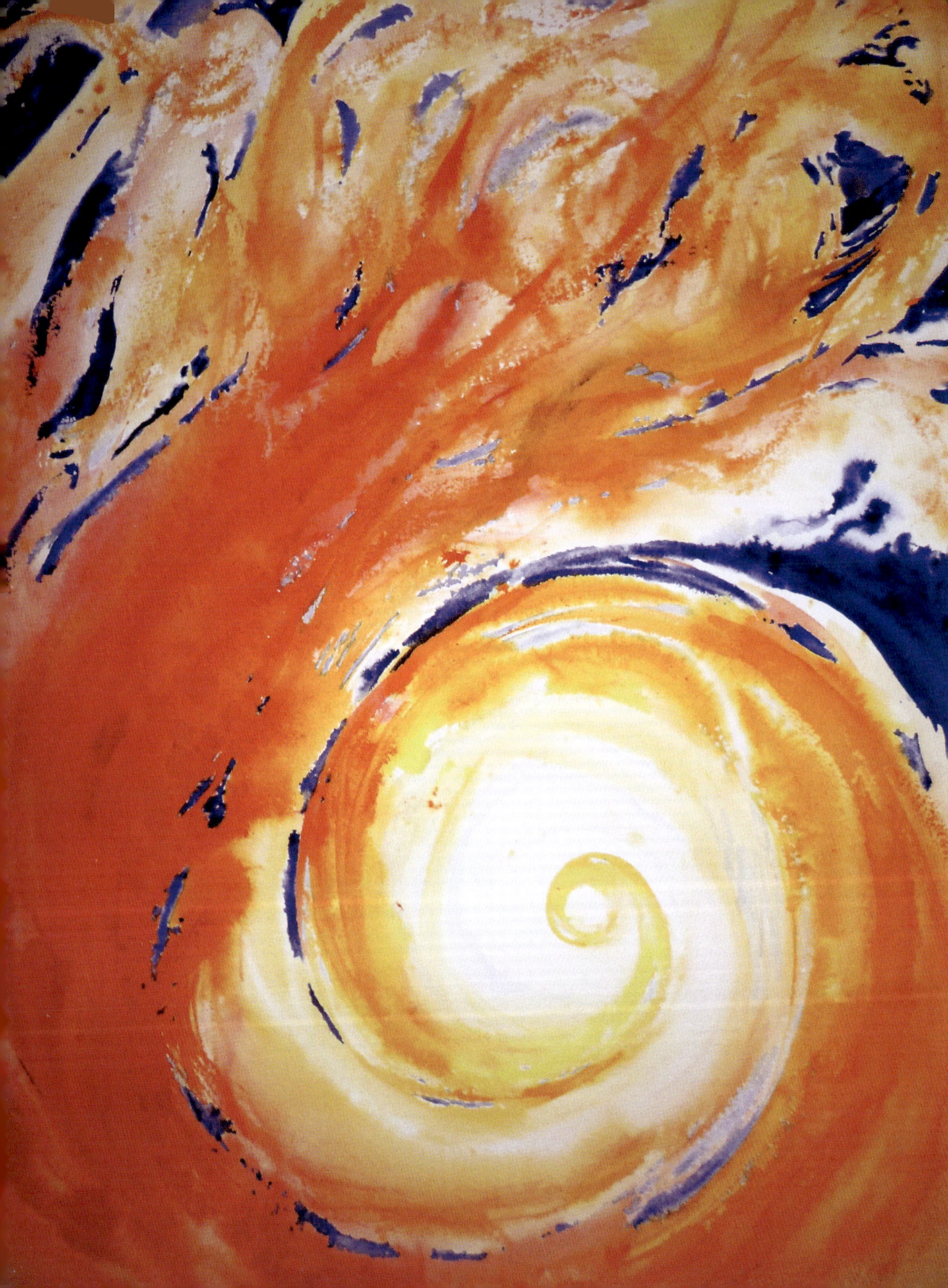

CREATIVE ENERGY

The spiral suggests primordial power, an immense explosion that continues to expand. As I con-template the macrocosm of celestial space and the microcosm of terrestrial atoms, I marvel at the brilliance of design. The contem-plation of birth and growth help me to accept other humans and to achieve my own integration.

Creative Energy:
31 x 24

DESTRUCTIVE POWER

The viral and dark forces wreak havoc upon our planet. Sometimes the negative energy is uncontrollable. I choose to push back against the knowable impulses that destroy the environment, damage others and lead to my own disintegration.

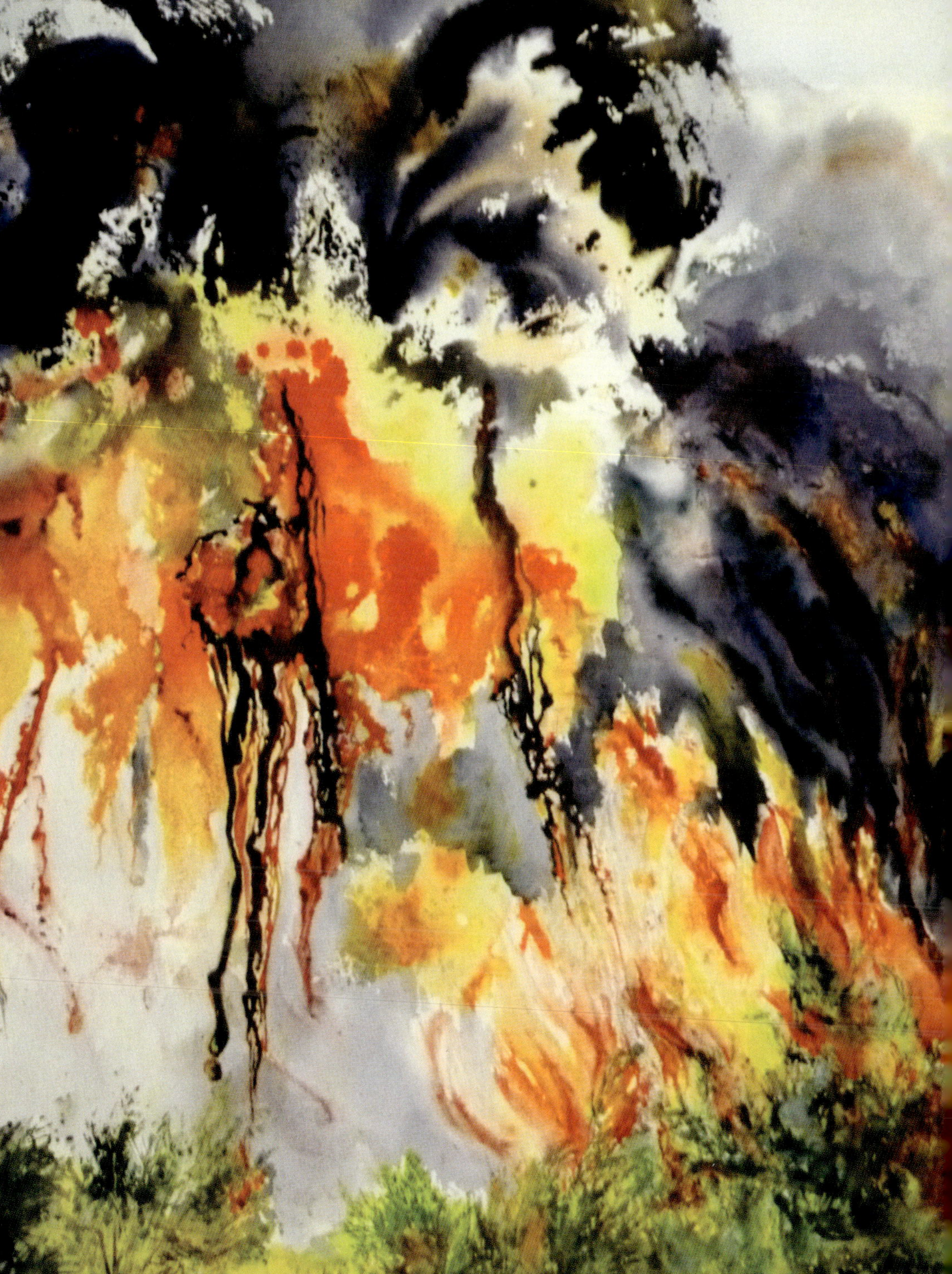

Destructive Energy:
31 x 24

LEONARD'S BROKEN LEG

Is getting a doctorate worth being away from my family all summer?

I am arguing with myself. My GI bill as a Korean War veteran is about to run out. How else can I support my family without a Doctor of Musical Arts in competitive academia? Is it fair for my wife, Elaine, to take care of three kids and a baby in humid Collegedale, Tennessee, while I sit near Boston working on this stupid degree?

My two solo recitals and one chamber music concert are successful. All of my comprehensive exams are finished, including the one I flunked the first time around. My French and German language tests are over.

The degree I am completing is a Doctor of Musical Arts in Piano Performance with a cognate in Art History. I am analyzing manuscripts of Schumann's piano music with a view to writing the first-ever paper on his variation techniques. The topic has been approved, and the first drafts accepted. This is the final critical typing. The handwritten music annotations need to be inserted and footnoted. The research then is validated with a lecture/recital of Schumann's composition in variation form or piano pieces heavily influenced by this form.

I sit on the porch, a clunky typewriter on my lap, messy carbon paper and correcting fluid handy. My friends, the Browns, are providing without charge a room in their South Lancaster home. A blue Ford I recognize turns into the driveway. My wife, Elaine, and our four children have driven the eight hundred miles from Tennessee to Massachusetts. It's a long way to drive in a car with no air conditioning.

Doors fly open. Kids come running. I hug Elaine with our new babe in arms while the three older ones cling to her skirts. For a while we have only tears without words. Then, in a torrent, I say, "You must be exhausted. How was the trip? Want a drink? Is Lowell over his cold? Maybe we can all stay here for the night, and then we…"

My hosts appear in the doorway to see what's going on. "You can stay right here," Mrs. Brown offers.

"We have some cots and sleeping bags," adds her husband, Ted.

My children have been well primed. "Daddy, we are here to help you finish your school," they say.

With the happy chatter of children playing in the background, I try to concentrate on document preparation. The restive kids do their best to be quiet while I peck on the portable typewriter.

The family settles into a home-away-from-home routine for a few days: the same porch, the same rattling typewriter, the same kids fighting among themselves or playing nicely. Suddenly I hear a thud. Silence from the ground six feet below. Screams from the banister above. Elaine rushes to pick up the frightened four-year old. I can see that his right leg is at a strange angle. "Don't lift him!" I firmly command. The skin is abraded, but I see no bad bleeding. We consult a nurse and decide it is safe to transport my son, Leonard, by car to the New England Sanitarium and Hospital some twenty-five miles away. In the emergency room a doctor examines and x-rays the leg. There is definitely one break and a green stick fracture. The orthopedist places a temporary plaster cast on the broken leg.

Back home, the gravity of the situation begins to sink in. I have to meet that deadline for my doctoral research thesis or else graduation is a year away. The next summer I will be away from my family again. No way. With laser beam focus I type the conclusions and paste in the musical illustrations. I finish the document on time.

Two days later, when I enter Leonard's hospital room, my son screams uncontrollably. I lean over his bed and hug him gently to assure him that everything will be all right. After a half hour his body relaxes. I smell the release of all fluids and solids. I push the call button. The nurse arrives. Her first words are, "I wish you wouldn't visit. He's so quiet and well behaved until you come."

"Has he eaten?" No answer. "Has he drunk any liquids?" Still no reply. "Bring some food and juice," I order. "I want to see his doctor."

While I await the doctor's visit, the nurse explains, "Leonard is a model patient. He doesn't complain or ask for anything."

"How long will it be before it is safe to travel eight hundred miles by car?

"I don't know; you'll have to consult the doctor," the nurse responds.

The orthopedic intern is reading his clipboard as he walks into the hospital room. "Let's see here. How's the little fellow doing?" he asks, glancing at the barely four-year-old boy with his foot in the air. "Are you his father?"

"Yes, sir. I appreciate what you are doing to fix his broken leg."

"Our plan is to take off this temporary cast and give him a sturdier one. Then the child—I see his name is Leonard—will have to get used to this traction for about six weeks." He shows me the blurry x-ray film and continues, "Here is the break, and there is the crack nearby. Our concern is that at only age four the good leg will grow faster than the injured one. That's why keeping the tension on the leg is so important."

"Does that mean that he will have to stay in the hospital for six weeks?" I ask.

"I'm afraid so. That's what we usually do."

"Dr. Livermore, is there any possibility of taking him home in a couple of days? The semester begins next week. I have a family of four young children and no place to stay in this vicinity. In addition, I simply can't afford the hospital bill."

The doctor replies, "I can understand your dilemma. But we can't take the risk of the leg healing improperly."

"You said that you plan to set the leg and put on the hard cast in a few days. What if I make traction possible while I take him home? I promise to see an orthopedist at the end of the two-day's drive."

Eagerly, I listen for his opinion. "Obviously, he can't stay here without his parents; the child is wasting away in this hospital environment. There is a window of time, short of a week, when the leg has not really begun to harden. After that period or time, it is important to have steady traction so that one leg does not end up shorter than the other."

"Thank you, sir. I will have my grandfather, who is a retired carpenter, make a proper frame. I promise to take him to an orthopedist immediately upon arrival in Chattanooga."

My grandfather Freiberger, who lives nearby, constructs a rectangular pallet with two upright supports and a crossbeam. I am cautious, but determined to make this work. On the way home, Elaine drives the car, and two kids sit in the front. The rig holding Leonard's leg up occupies two-thirds of the back seat. I hold the baby alongside the pallet. Along the way we stop overnight at a friend's house. With improvised mosquito netting over the windows, I sleep in the car with Leonard. Inwardly I am fearful that I may have made a wrong decision.

As I promised the doctor, I seek medical help immediately upon my return to Tennessee. Before we even go to our home I stop to see an orthopedist in Chattanooga. His eyes widen when Leonard arrives ensconced in the contraption. "I've never seen anything like this, he says." As the doctor examines his leg, Leonard plays about happily.

"Take him home," the doctor says. "That's the best place. I'll see him in a couple of weeks."

Day and night everything in Leonard's world takes place on that padded pallet. Night and day our family includes him in the near normal activities. I have taken a huge, calculated risk and I am so glad that my son's legs match. At about the same time as Leonard gets out of traction, I hear that my doctorate is secure. Far more important to me, my son's leg has healed with no sign of a limp.

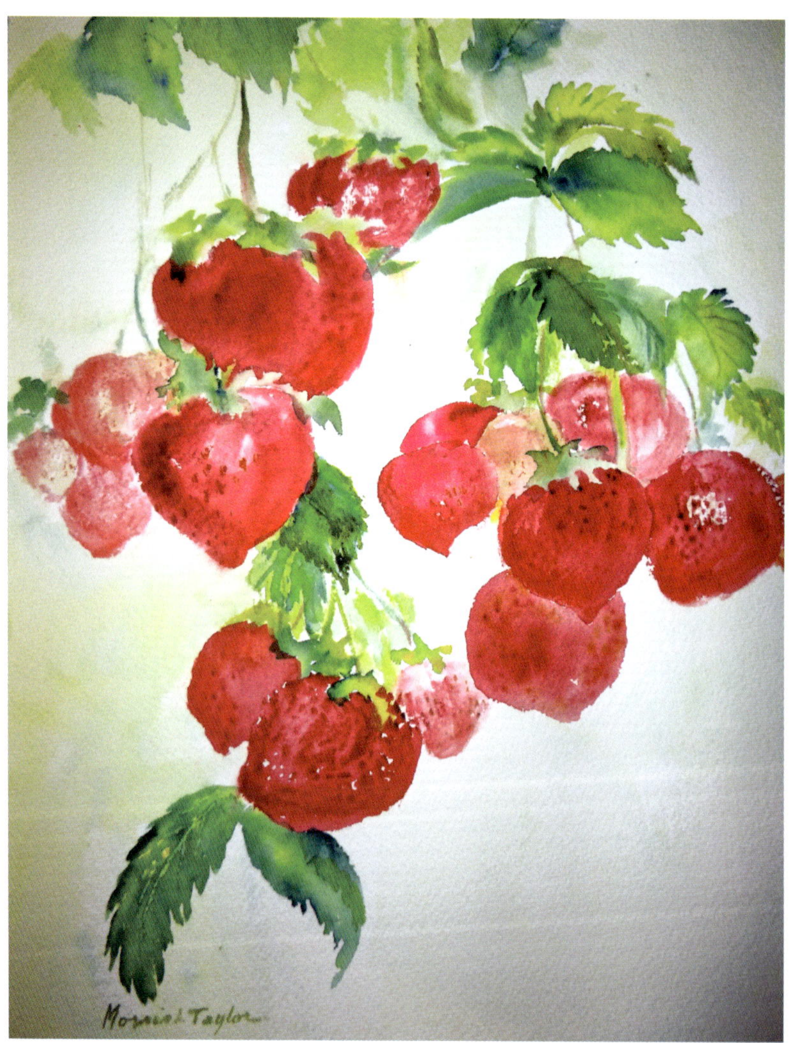

Picking Strawberries, 12x9

MY MUSICAL LOVE AFFAIR

I am chair of the Division of Fine Arts at Southern Missionary College in Collegedale, Tennessee. The school farm fills the narrow valley. The school buildings perch on the surrounding hillside. Many students pay tuition by working in the broom factory or Little Debbie's cookie business. Faculty and students are expected to exemplify the conservative life-style of the Adventist Church.

I need a cultural and career challenge. I have a doctoral degree. Now I have four children, ages two to seven years of age. I have matured as a pianist, educator and chairman. I become restless in this small community and yearn for a breakout experience to further my musical career.

My mind goes back to my graduate student years at Boston University. I had just turned twenty when I received a Bachelor of Arts degree in music from Atlantic Union College. I am enrolled for a Master's degree in performance at Boston University, but I feel like a beginning piano student.

Soon after I enroll at B. U., I save enough money to attend a recital by my hero, Dame Myra Hess. The lights dim in Boston's Symphony Hall. A hush creeps over the audience. Into the spotlight from stage right emerges a lady of noble mien. Her confident bearing makes up for her short stature. She wears her hair pulled back over her ears in a trademark bun. She floats elegantly across the stage expanse toward the piano. After a gracious smile and pleasant nod, the pianist seats herself discretely in front of the keyboard of a nine-foot, concert Steinway. So gracious is her English demeanor, I can almost smell the scent of Earl Grey tea and crumpets with marmalade.

Dame Myra Hess opens the musical score on the piano rack. Those first notes of sunshine! The melody spins as purely as a *bel canto* singer; the accompaniment purrs like a nuanced string quartet. Throughout the first movement of Schubert's *Sonata in A, Opus 120*, I feel suspended like a dragonfly in the sun's rays. The development section with scale-like passages alternating with brilliant chords feels majestically festive under Dame Myra's effortless hands.

The slower andante is gossamer. I admire the perfect serenity with which she caresses the keys. The melodic threads shine like silk in moonlight: delicate shadows for the notes borrowed from the minor key, a glint of candlelight for the major key.

Then the stars come out. In the third movement the tempo rollicks along with cascading scales and leaping arpeggios like falling water splashing. I revel in the clarity and brilliance of her sensitive touch. My new musical heroine enthralls me.

Myra Hess allows the natural weight of her arms to fall gently upon the keys of the piano. This produces a warm resonant sound pleasing to the ear. Dame Myra is England's greatest pianist and the leading exponent of the Tobias Matthay method of piano playing. I dream of one day studying with her. By contrast many virtuoso pianists of the day subscribe to the Theodor Leschetizky method whose exponents played brilliantly but with a more brittle, harsher tone. On the inspiration of Dame Myra's concert, I determine to be the best pianist I can possibly become no matter how hard I must practice.

My reverie ends. I return to the reality of my need to get away from this isolated valley and the routine of a small religious school. Although the professor exchange movement has barely begun in academic circles and is unheard of in church related colleges, I determine to pursue this idea. Self-doubt leads me to ask myself, *Would this world class pianist, Myra Hess, even grant an audition, let alone accept me as a student?* Before I can change my mind, I write a short, sincere letter addressed to Dame Myra Hess, care of the Royal Academy of Music, London, England.

Within a fortnight I receive a handwritten letter from her secretary, Anita Gunn, "Madame is pleased to arrange an audition upon your arrival in Great Britain."

I will make this happen. But how? My family depends on the meager salary at Southern Missionary College, and I have no savings. This is not a time for dithering. I discover a sister institution, Newbold College. Their music professor, Roy Scarr, agrees to a one year swapping of jobs, salaries, homes and cars. I persuade the presidents of both colleges to accept the proposition. My school offers me a thousand and two hundred dollar travel allowance, but for other expenses, I am on my own. My wife Elaine goes along with the plan even though she knows there will be considerable financial sacrifice. The children agree with age-appropriate enthusiasm.

In August of 1963 I drive to New York, park our Dodge station wagon for my counterpart to pick up, and board the SS America. We six set sail for Southampton, England. I feel so fortunate. Our family occupies the biggest room in second class, deep in the bowels of the largest passenger vessel to cross the Atlantic. Our cabin has two double beds, plus a cot and an extra crib. By special arrangement with the purser, I am granted permission to practice on a grand piano in the First Class section at five a.m. each morning when the main bar is empty.

We finally arrive at our temporary home in Popeswood Lodge, the actual home of the poet, Alexander Pope. The building is now divided into apartments.

True to her promise, Dame Myra receives me at her home in St. Johnswood near the famous cricket field, northwest of London. The manor house sits amidst an elegant garden. The interior blends antiques with tasteful Art Deco furniture. A German Steinway piano dominates the drawing room. Dame Myra enters, gracious as the Queen of England. She invites me to be seated on the concert bench. My hands feel stiff and clammy; I discretely warm my fingers. The first notes I play for her are Schubert's *Sonata In A Major, Op. 120*, the same composition from her Symphony Hall recital a decade before. I explain my goal to become a good pianist so that I may be an excellent teacher. I ask if she can recommend a tutor during the year of my exchange professorship.

Dame Myra appears to have the world dumped on her shoulders. She leans on the piano and looks into my eyes. "I never recommend anyone. You see in my position…" her voice trails off. After a pause she says, "Tell Robin Wood at the Royal Academy that I sent you. When he gives me word, I will hear you play again." After a few intense lessons with Mr. Wood, I ask if he will recommend that I play for Dame Myra. He agrees to phone her secretary to make an appointment.

Seven more times I have the privilege of studying with this titan of pianism. I arrive in the early afternoon and continue until teatime. Dame Myra, a person of German Jewish descent, was knighted Dame of the British Empire in 1941. During the Second World War she returned to England from America in U-boat infested waters and organized morale-building concerts at noon during the blitz at the unheated and art empty National Gallery of Art. For six and a half years she organized these concerts for persons who had to remain in the capitol during the buzz bombing rather than flee to the English countryside.

During my last meeting with my beloved mentor, Elaine and I give Dame Myra a homemade loaf of anadama bread that includes molasses and cornmeal. With both of her arthritic hands she places it on her piano, "My dear," she says, "you don't know what this means to me. They always give me cake, and I prefer bread." The generosity of her soul matches the beauty of her music.

During the time I am in England as an exchange professor, I not only fulfill my professorial responsibilities for music and art classes and for choral conducting, but I also diligently practice the piano in my studio. My wife, Elaine, is teaching half time and caring for the children. We have the help of a live-in nanny, a college student, JoAnn, who lives with us without charge in return for some childcare. I decide before we leave that I will fulfill a lifetime dream and make my professional debut as a pianist at London's famed Wigmore Hall.

In October, I gin up enough courage to visit Wigmore Hall. I ask to speak to the manager. She shows me the auditorium. I am thrilled to peek into the Renaissance-style concert hall built at the turn into the twentieth century. I realize that in this space the world's great musicians perform, including two of my pianist idols, Artur Rubenstein and Myra Hess. Young artists also make their first professional appearance in London at this location, because a good critical review in this cultural capitol can be very useful in launching a musical career.

"Ma'am, I would like to make arrangements for a debut piano concert," I say. "Would there be a date available this season?" We settle on Sunday afternoon at three o'clock, May 24, 1964. I sign the lease agreement.

Tucking in a wisp of graying hair and adjusting her pince-nez, the lady replies, "This may be possible. Come with me to the office and we will look at the schedule. Who is your manager?"

"I don't have a manager. Is this absolutely necessary? I am an exchange professor at a church-related college in Bracknell. My wife and four children are living on a missionary wage."

"Well, it would be an unusual arrangement. Maybe it would be possible."

"I need your recommendations regarding the printing of programs and tickets," I say.

"That is no problem," says the manager. "If you

provide your own ushers, I can reduce the fee. You will need to use our stage person for the lights and our ticket person for the box office. There is a form customary for the program. Here are some samples. Contact Vail & Co. Ltd. on Leeke Street. They also have the format for printing the five hundred and forty-five tickets."

I think I'd better attend a concert at Wigmore Hall soon to understand the protocol, what the performers wear and how the audience reacts. I wonder if the music critics will attend my recital?

The next Saturday night I take the bus from Popeswood Lodge to Wigmore Hall in downtown London. A young cellist is playing his debut recital. The concert goes well. I am particularly pleased with the magnificent acoustics of this world-famous chamber music venue. The next day I purchase *The Times* newspaper and eagerly locate the concert review. "A cellist without a tone," begins the critique, "is like Sampson without his hair." The body of the article is a mixed review of the performance. The close states that if this young artist is serious about his career, he should hire an accompanist other than his mother. After reading that account, I choose not to read any other reviews until after my own recital in May.

For the piano program that I plan for my debut recital, I will open the performance with Schubert's *Sonata in A major, Opus 120*. I will continue with J. S. Bach's *French Suite in G Major*, the piece Dame Myra played at Carnegie Hall when she returned to America after the World War II. I plan to close the first half of the program with Schumann's *Etudes Symphoniques*, one of the pivotal works in variation form that I had analyzed for my Doctor of Musical Arts degree from Boston University. After the intermission I choose to perform three twentieth century works,—*Decorations* by the Englishman, John Ireland, and *Three Page Sonata* by the American, Charles Ives, and to conclude the program, I will play the brilliant suite of pieces by Claude Debussy, *Pour le Piano*.

Six months seems far away. I know that having chosen a challenging program suitable for a debut, I have to prepare meticulously. I initiate a daily schedule that involves physical exercise, a nourishing diet and fastidious piano practice. In a second-hand shop I find a concert outfit with tails, white tie and cummerbund. The program goes to the printers early so that it doubles as a publicity flier. I borrow a better typewriter to write official looking invitations to the London papers that may choose to print a notice. The music critics receive a special letter that includes complimentary tickets for the best seats in the house.

In the whirl of activities leading up to the debut, I loose myself in the music. Everything in my life centers around being faithful to the printed music score. I know that I have started my piano career late in life and with decided disadvantages. In spite of this, I am determined to be the best pianist that I can be. This is the fulfillment of a life-long dream.

The day before the concert is my Sabbath Day. I cannot practice; instead I worship and rest. Early Sunday I rehearse the program, this time on the German Steinway in the concert hall. I marvel at the beauty of tone, the evenness of touch and the perfection of the acoustics.

In the Green Room backstage, in which artists of the past century have lingered, I pray for the blessing of Divine Power. All earthly cares are set aside. As I stride to the piano for the performance, I feel an inner peace. The bright lights hide the audience from view. I exist for the music. The two hours seem as an eternity, yet the time passes quickly. Soon I am playing the last encore, *Three Scottish Dances,* written by Chopin when he was discouraged by his own piano performances in Scotland. Like Chopin, I choose to remember the happy times no matter what the critics say the next day.

On Monday morning I have a class at seven-thirty. Someone had already found the review in *The Times* of London and posted it on the bulletin board. I peruse it quickly on the way to the classroom, and then try to concentrate on my teaching. With deep satisfaction I read the review. I believe that the critic is fair in pointing out both my weaknesses and strengths as an aspiring pianist still in my early thirties.

THE TIMES, LONDON 25 MAY 1964

PIANIST WITH SENSE OF STYLE

Schumann's Symphonic Studies are a frequent visitor to the Wigmore Hall, oddly for so heroically proportioned a work; and, in fact few of the pianists who attempt it have the interpretative stature to do it full justice, though one can recall any number of valiant failures. Mr. Morris Taylor's comparative success with the work at his recital yesterday afternoon was quite surprising, as he had opened with a gracious but flaccid account of Schubert's *A major Sonata, opus 120*, which suggest that his métier lay in small things. The Schumann was not without technical lapses, but Mr. Taylor showed a fine judgment of scale in balancing the declamatory and contemplative elements of the music.

To this, also, he matched excellent performances of three twentieth-century works, and particularly a tense account of Charles Ives's hauntingly disharmonious *Three Page Sonata*. Debussy's *Pour le Piano* received a clean, crisp reading, which, in spite of the splendid Schumann, confirmed an earlier impression, left by some beautifully poised playing in Bach's *French G major Suite*, that Mr. Taylor is a pianist whose major assets are a strong sense of style and graciousness of touch.

A GRACEFUL TRILOGY

BOTTICELLI AT THE UFFIZI

Snow and dust swirl in intricate patterns
over ancient pavement worn by pilgrims
like me questing for truth in equilibrium.

Sandro, you and I are alone together;
my life dream come true to confront with you
crystalline beauty and dirty truth.

In London and Washington we first met,
but now in your hometown Florence
I am enervated by your virtuosic elegance.

With you I celebrate at the altar of beauty,
the mysteries of immaculate creation
commingling with human sophistry.

You and I believe in divine origins
and explore nature and philosophy—
pudgy divine child reaching for our fingers.

Consummate artist, through the prism of your eye
I view the colorful portrait and spectral vision
of my existence. Magnificat. Requiescat.

X-RAYED ANALYSIS OF BOTTICELLI'S PAINTINGS

X-RAYED ANALYSIS

Charming grace
dancing in place
on painterly surface.

Through laconic smile
melancholy hearts beguile
in magnificent style.

Ladies are waiting
tousled hair plaiting
some courtiers sating.

Prestige will enhance
with warrior lance
and Platonic romance.

While aggrandizing self
men display wealth
to cover their stealth.

Ignore the poor peasant
and dine on some pheasant
to make life more pleasant.

The church will support
the luxuries you import
for your family cohort.

Penance is ample
shine of the apple
by building a chapel.

Eternal flame ignite
the flickering light
of a soul's last rite.

PERFECT PAINTING

Mystical melodrama
intoxicates my nostrils
with pungent incense.

Vibrant pastel color
enlarges my retina
to perceive the spectral.

Undulating dance
coordinates my muscular
response in rhythm.

Pearlescent skin
incites a sensual desire
to touch worshipfully.

Luminous body radiance
activates corporeal beings
search for intrinsic worth.

Heavenly vision
ignites earthly passion
for Renaissance perfection.

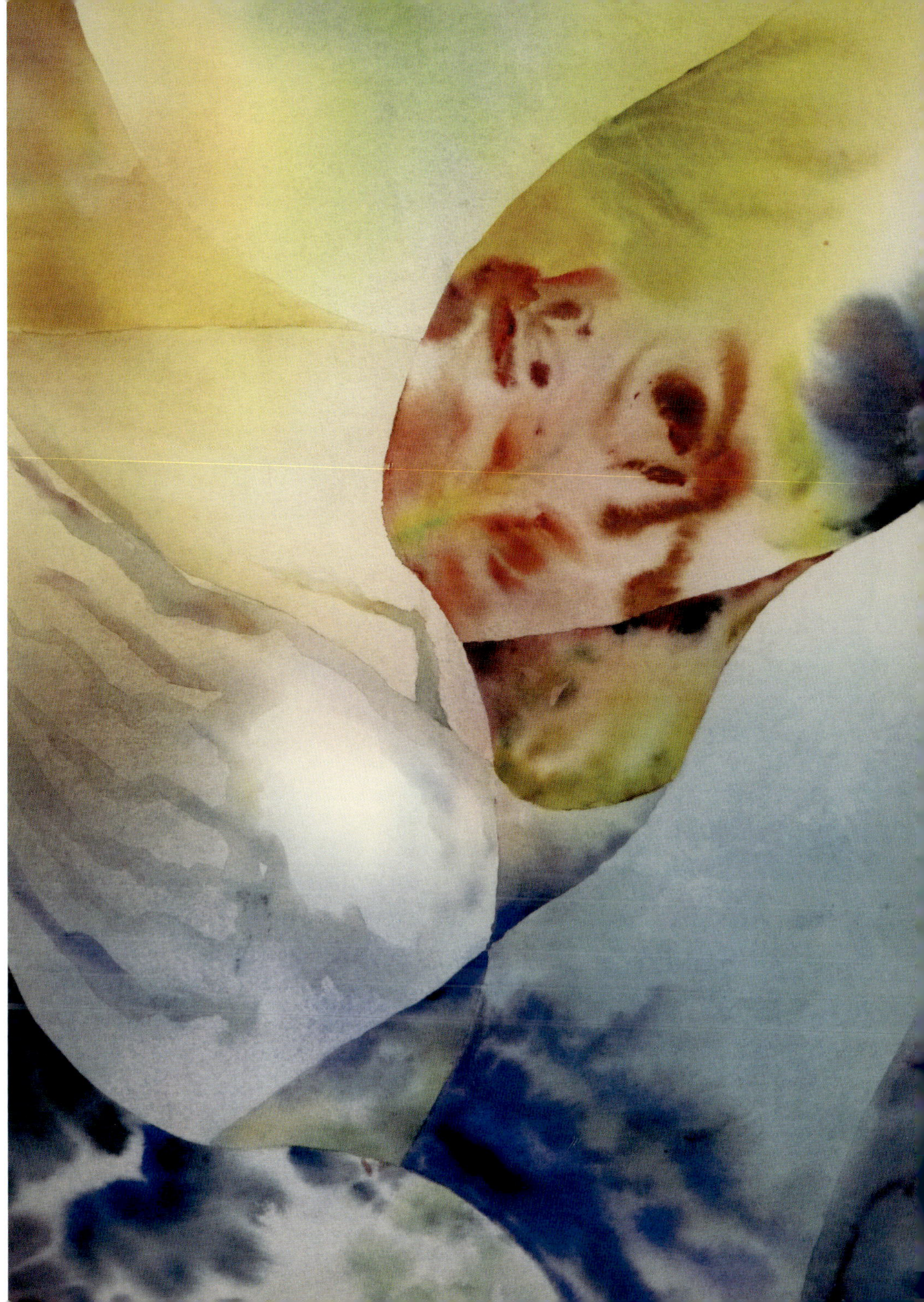

Graceful Sea Images,
20x16

DON'T MOCK MY BIRD

"Tell me a story about when you were a little boy," the children beg.

Since Easter is approaching, I tell my four children about my grandfather's chickens. He taught me how to pump water from the well, to gather the eggs and to fill the grain feeders. The kids listen attentively.

"Why can't we have some chickens?" they ask.

"Maybe we can," I reply. "You'll have to learn how to take care of the fragile baby chicks."

After a considerable search, I find a farmer near our home in Collegedale, Tennessee, who has fertilized eggs for sale. I surprise Lucy, age seven; Leonard, six; Lowell, five; and Lyndon, two and a half; with the gift of a dozen fertilized eggs.

"These are special eggs," I explain, "There is a daddy chicken called a rooster and a mommy chicken called a hen. It takes both of them to make an egg that will turn into a baby chicken."

"How do you know which one is a daddy?" Lucy asks.

"Well, the daddy rooster has a comb, like a big red hat. And the mommy hen is a smaller bird with less fancy feathers. The mommy lays the eggs."

"What does the rooster do?"

"We'll talk about that when the chicks hatch."

"What's hatch?"

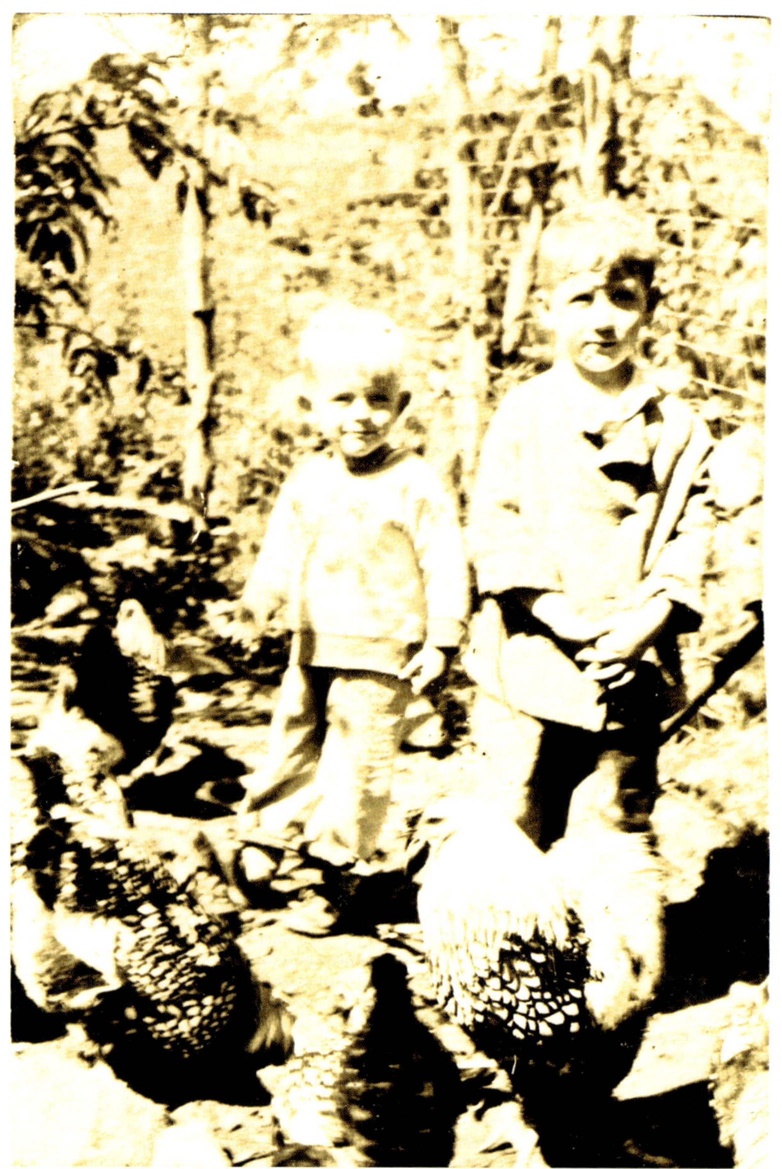

Morris and Skippy in the Hen Yard

"We have to wait and see. It will be three weeks until the baby chicks come out of the eggshells."

The children watch me place the eggs gently onto a soft towel. The low heat atop the open oven door creates a uniform temperature. "Two times a day you can help me turn the eggs carefully," I say.

In about three weeks, Lucy comes running. "I hear the chicky. He's making a hole. Will he come out?"

The two older boys race to get in on the excitement. Lyndon is not far behind.

"You can watch, but do not touch."

"Look, I can see the mouth!"

"There's another one pecking."

"The egg is cracking open."

"I can see the head!"

"This one's all wet."

"Don't worry; the baby will dry in the warmth from the oven." Then I explain how the fuzz will turn into feathers in a few weeks.

"Daddy, she's touching the chicky."

"I did not. He did."

"Stop fighting. Daddy needs you to take care of the baby chickens. Who wants to help?"

Eagerly everyone dances about the hatching brood. Each child gets a special task and learns how to be responsible for fragile pets. With gentle care the chicks outgrow the small box and the larger enclosure in the kitchen. They become part of the family.

The next month is exciting. I construct a pen under the house from old fencing wire with small mesh. It's hard for children to understand that as the ten surviving birds grow bigger, they begin to stink and will have to live outdoors.

We live in a residential area on an acre of land with room for a garden and small woods where the children can play. I especially like the birds on our property. Our resident mockingbird has a repertoire of about fifteen songs that imitate most of the local wild species.

One night tragedy strikes the hen-yard. When I go to feed the flock, a young female hen, called a pullet, is missing. Two days later a rooster disappears without a trace. When the third chicken is not on the perch at night, I grow alarmed. I am determined to find the culprit that is stealing our chickens. I feel betrayed when I see evidence that the neighbor's dog is the sly thief, one meal per day.

Striding across the street, I knock on the dog owner's front door, determined to demand that he banish his dog. "Good morning, Jim. Did you know …?"

"Quiet please," he interrupts, "my wife had a really bad night. Molly's still is sleeping."

"Is she not well?"

"Molly is having it rough. I guess we've kept it pretty much to ourselves." After a big sigh he continues, "Close to the last stages of cancer." We both tear up and hug.

Sadly I conclude there is only one solution for the case of the missing chickens. At breakfast I have a talk with the children.

"You know, the lady across the street is very sick. Mrs. Christianson needs the dog to keep her company. Maybe her dog will help her feel better. Shall we let the nice lady play with her pet?" When I sense that the children understand, I describe a plan. "I'll see if our friends, the Hefferlins, will take the chickens to their farm. Our chickens will be safe there." Dr. Ray Hefferlin is a lead researcher at the atomic labs at Oak Ridge, Tennessee. He is also head of the Physics Department at Southern Missionary College where I am teaching.

The children help me catch the remaining seven, put them in crates and transport them a mile away. Knowing we can visit the brood of chickens consoles them.

The next morning I get up early to tend my vegetable and flower garden. The bucket, spade and hoe rattle in the wheelbarrow as it bumps along. Suddenly, I hear the call of a chicken. I search to no avail. I am reminded of how much I miss the chickens that have become part of our family.

Again, I do my garden routine while the dew still lingers. The clucking of a missing chicken is more distinct this time. I am sure that I can follow the sound and catch the straggler. No luck. I feel frustrated.

The third morning, same thing. I am mystified. I say to myself, *You sentimental old coot. You must be going senile. I'm going to prove ...*

In mid-thought I look upward in the direction of the squawk. Up the tree, on this branch ... no, a bit higher on that branch. There, at the top of the tall tulip tree, is a mockingbird pretending to be a chicken. Mystery solved!

I tell the story to the children that night. We all laugh out loud. Of course, every child has to hear the mockingbird charade. When the tools in the wheelbarrow rattle, the mockingbird gets the cue. Time for the mockingbird to launch into the imitation chicken selection from his repertoire.

This is the song I would like to sing back to this bird who mocks my chickens:

> My dear faux raven, you're so craven.
> You falsifying hen, I'll get out my pen;
> with wicked scoff I'll write you off.
> A vocal audition? On one condition:
> Practice your song; your pitch is wrong.
> You'll never replace real chickens.

The final days of Mrs. Christianson are as comfortable as possible. Her beloved dog is by her side until her passing. The chickens grow to become egg-laying hens and proud roosters to the delight of the Taylor children. The mockingbird sings on.

.

Hen Hatching Eggs, ►
12×16

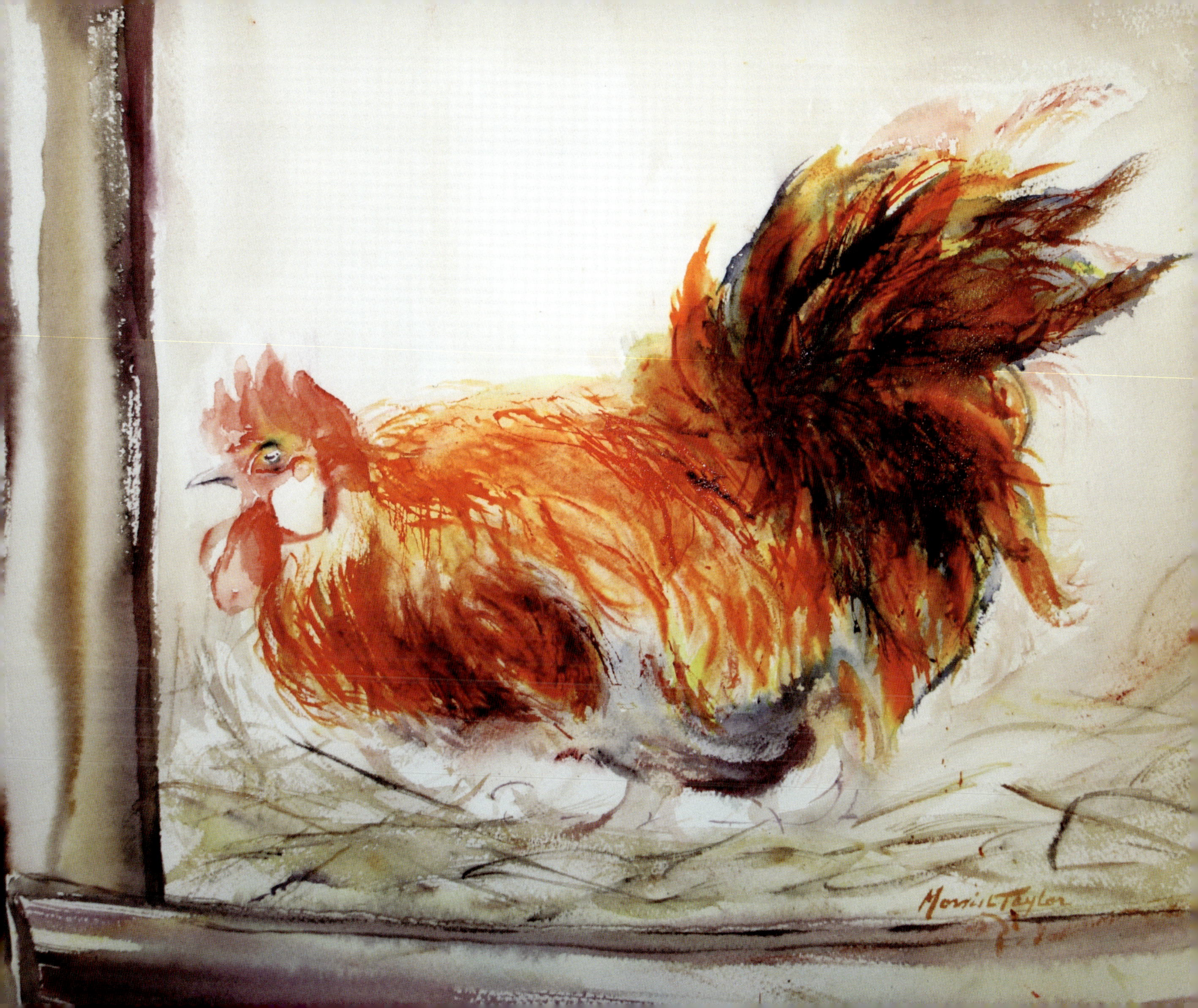
Morris Taylor

OBSTINANT ANGEL

In winter, Aspen, Colorado, is a chic ski resort. In summer, the town becomes the temporary home of world-class musicians. In July of 1968, I am attending the Aspen Institute with the express purpose of studying piano with Madame Rosina Lhevinne. During the academic year, she reigns as the empress of pianists at the Juilliard School in New York City. Summers she teaches at the Aspen Institute. Even though this is the third summer that I have the privilege of coaching with Madame Lhevinne, I am still in awe. I wish I could adequately express my appreciation for her extraordinary mentoring.

This particular afternoon, when I knock on the door of Mme. Lhevinne's cottage, Sarah, the maid, meets me.

"Mr. Taylor, Madame is not well today. Your lesson will be postponed," she informs me.

"I hope it is nothing serious. Do you think that Madame Lhevinne would like to see me? Perhaps I can help," I say.

In a few minutes Sarah returns. "Yes, she will welcome you. The bedroom door is on the right."

"Doctors don't make house calls these days," the Madame complains as I enter the room.

In my best bedside manner I inquire of her health.

"I have a headache and my knees hurt." Otherwise the ninety-year-old lady seems okay.

"Sarah," I say, "Do you have some ice and towels?"

Presently she brings them. I make a comfortable compress for my beloved teacher's head.

"Please bring me a kettle of hot water and more towels." I prepare a heating compress for her ailing knee joints.

Pleasant talk and hydrotherapy make the patient more comfortable. In about an hour my beloved piano coach gently closes her eyes in slumber. On subsequent visits I help, though Sarah learns to manage the treatment without my assistance.

Meanwhile, I write to my wife Elaine in Angwin, California, requesting her to mail our Thermaphore. This safe heating pad plugs into the electricity administering moist heat to aching joints without the mess of water and towels.

When I return for my scheduled piano lesson during one of the predictable afternoon rainstorms in this high altitude resort town, Madame honors me with a long and intense piano lesson. I can tell that she is tired. I turn to leave.

"Do you have time to write a few letters for me?" she asks.

"Yes, Ma'am," I reply, eager to show my appreciation.

At two the next afternoon she is ready to dictate the first letter. "Mr. Taylor, write to Battle Creek, Michigan, to buy one of those heating pads."

"Madame, I can't write that letter. The one you have is a gift."

Her obvious frustration betrays the fact that the Madame is not accustomed to anyone contradicting her. After an awkward pause, she asserts, "Mr. Taylor, you are such an obstinate angel!"

A month later I receive a message from Madame Lhevinne. Another student had written the thank you note. Included in the envelope is a blank check with her shaky signature. I keep this document as a cherished possession along with a signed photo of Madame Lhevinne inscribed, "To Morris Taylor, the kindest and most intelligent man I ever met."

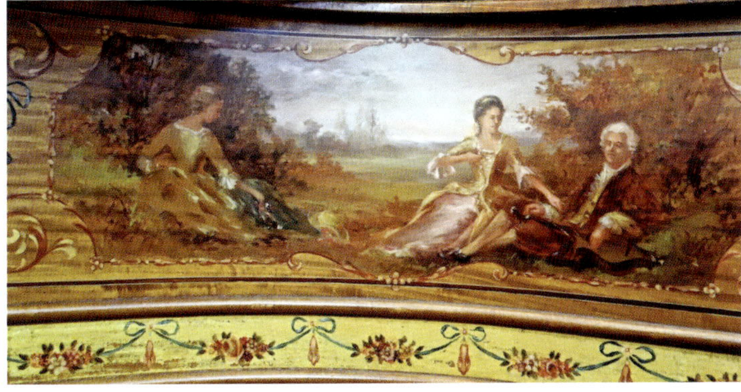

Morris's seven-foot Steinway piano was built and decorated in 1897. The original case was hand painted by Arthur Blackmore, who preceded by J. Burr Tiffany for twenty years, as head of Steinway Art Department. A similar piano that belonged to Cole Porter is still being played at the Waldorf-Astoria Hotel in New York City.

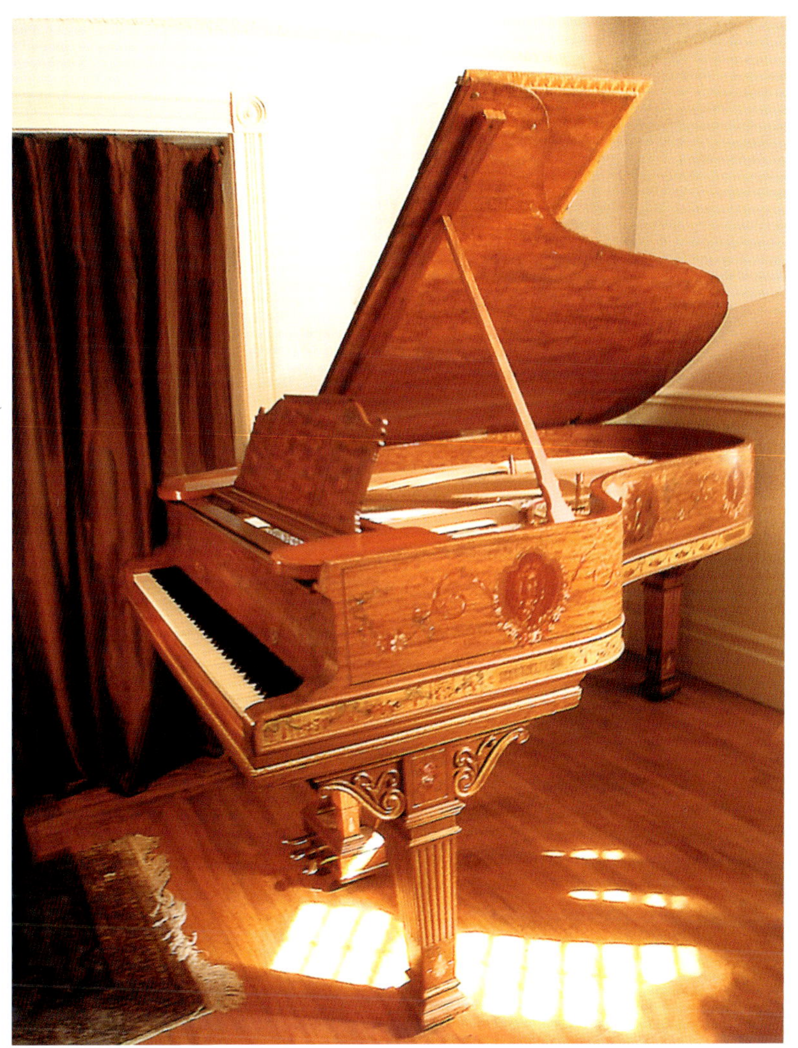

JUANITA'S WOODEN LEG

"Why don't y'all set a spell. It's too hot to be standin' in the sun."

Juanita is being her hospitable self. She lives in an unpainted, wood frame house with a corrugated tin roof. Though working in the sun-drenched fields gnarls her face and hands from scratching the soil with hand tools, her round face shines with a warm smile and bashful dimples. At first she seems overweight. Hard work and raising a family keep her muscles well toned. My wife and I wish we could make her work easier and her life better.

"I'm here to invite you to a Bible storytelling. I think your family will like the singing too." My wife, Elaine, points to Juanita's brood of young children who cling to their mother's skirts.

"My kids like stories," says Juanita as she hides part of her face with a timid gesture.

After a pause Elaine says, "Mighty pretty looking girls, you have there. I think they'll enjoy the meeting."

"Got nine of them," Juanita proudly answers.

"No boys?"

"No, Ma'am." Juanita points to a bend in the road. "Just a no-good husband. Always out with the boys that's huntin' coon or drinkin' whiskey. Girls, fetch these younguns a drink." Juanita gestures toward the well.

With a dipper, two of the girls fill dusty cups from the bucket. Eagerly the sweaty Taylor kids drink up. A quick glance assesses the situation. The well is too close to the outdoor toilet. One must be polite so, sadly, Elaine does not interfere. In a few days all four Taylor children have stomachaches and the go-quicks. It is not serious, but they're miserable. Everyone feels better by the next Saturday afternoon, however, the appointed time for the story hour.

Juanita lives in a wooded area the locals call "Grasshopper." In the 1960s only a few hunters and campers venture into these parts. The scattered families tend to keep to themselves. Many are suspicious. Feuds fester. The residents eke out a living by subsistence farming, cultivating vegetables such as tomatoes, okra, sweet potatoes and beans. A few men have jobs in the nearby town of Birchwood. Poverty prevails. Health care is scarce. Folks in Southern Appalachia are spunky, secretive and skeptical.

Brother Baker, Sister Grace, and my wife, Elaine, join me and the members of my Sabbath School Class in teaching people of this isolated town how to improve their lives. Many of the men in Grasshopper are shiftless and have poor work habits leaving the women and children to fend for themselves. Booze is prevalent. Religion in that secluded valley often involves a literal interpretation of the Bible, including snake handling. Even law enforcement agents hardly dare to penetrate the area for fear of ambush.

While we are doing our weekly missionary visit, Juanita tells me this story. On a hot, humid summer day Big Bertha, a large young lady, is attending a secretive all-day meeting. The elders are arrayed on the platform at the front with cages of rattlesnakes. The faithful are seated in pews toward the front. Bertha stands just behind a rope that cordon off the rest of the people who are curious, local on-lookers. Young people wander over the grounds or hang from trees to see goings-on through the windows. Some ne'er-do-well spits on his finger and slides it upward on Bertha's bare legs. She lets out an ungodly scream. Instead of interrupting the meeting, the believers wave their arms and shout "Amen." Big Bertha has the Spirit. A poisonous snake bites one of the preachers. The most ardent believers take him to his bed in the upper floor of his home where they pray for his healing. One by one, people are dismissed, as the prayers prove ineffective. He dies without medical help.

From Southern Missionary College, through Ooltewah— Owl's Nest in the language of the Native Americans who roamed here— to Grasshopper is eighteen miles. Some church volunteers and I drive from Collegedale, Tennessee, to Grasshopper near the Chickamauga Reservoir. We fix up the shack on the South side of the dirt road for Bible classes by repairing the tarpaper roof and by building a bridge over the dry creek in case of a downpour. A friend loans us a clunky piano, which we haul into the building for the singing.

On the north side of the road there is a combination gas station and grocery store with a tumbledown storage barn behind it. On the south side sits the small abandoned building that I rent for the Bible class. Rumor has it that there is a speakeasy where you can purchase bootleg liquor at the back. I am quite sure this is true, because my children and I have been scared away by shotgun fire when we were hiking. I do not dare to venture there; only folks known to the proprietor are allowed.

On the specified Saturday morning the Taylor family attends church at the Collegedale Tabernacle, a quarter mile down Camp Road where we live. I teach the adult Bible class and coach each person for their assigned role for the opening meeting in Grasshopper that afternoon. I advise, "Don't overdress and be friendly."

That afternoon quite a few Grasshopper locals, mostly women and children, gingerly enter the building that we have repaired, and sit on folding chairs. Elaine leads familiar gospel songs while I play the piano. I read a few favorite Bible texts. Prayers are short because mischievous eyes are open. The stories are the favorite item on the program, especially if they have action or violence like in the movies.

As a result of a year and many months more of Bible Studies, several of the people in Grasshopper decide to be baptized. Members of my adult Bible class at Southern Missionary College make detailed arrangements for the special occasion.

The water of Harrison Bay is seldom so blue as it is the day of the baptism. High cumulus clouds provide little shade. Brother Baker, a lay preacher who has assisted in the Branch Sabbath School, wades into the waist-deep water. Believers solemnly sing hymns on the banks of the dammed-up river. A group of candidates for baptism by immersion fidget in their white robes.

Juanita lingers near me. She appears to be calm and

resolute. Suddenly she grabs onto my arm vigorously. I almost fall down with the weight of this rather large woman. I gasp out loud when she hands me her wooden leg, stocking and shoe included!

With all the gravity I can muster, I lay the fabricated leg gently on the beach. I steady Juanita as she hops into the symbolic grave of baptism. Mud slimes through the toes of our bare feet. Goose bumps remind us of water not yet warmed by summer sun. My heart is clean and warm. Juanita and I have religion.

When Juanita believes that she can trust us, she admits that her husband shot off her leg during a drunken brawl. Many such tales, including this one, are true in Southern Appalachia. My wife and I continue a friendship with Juanita and her girls for many years. Our four kids prepare presents at Christmas time for Juanita and her nine daughters.

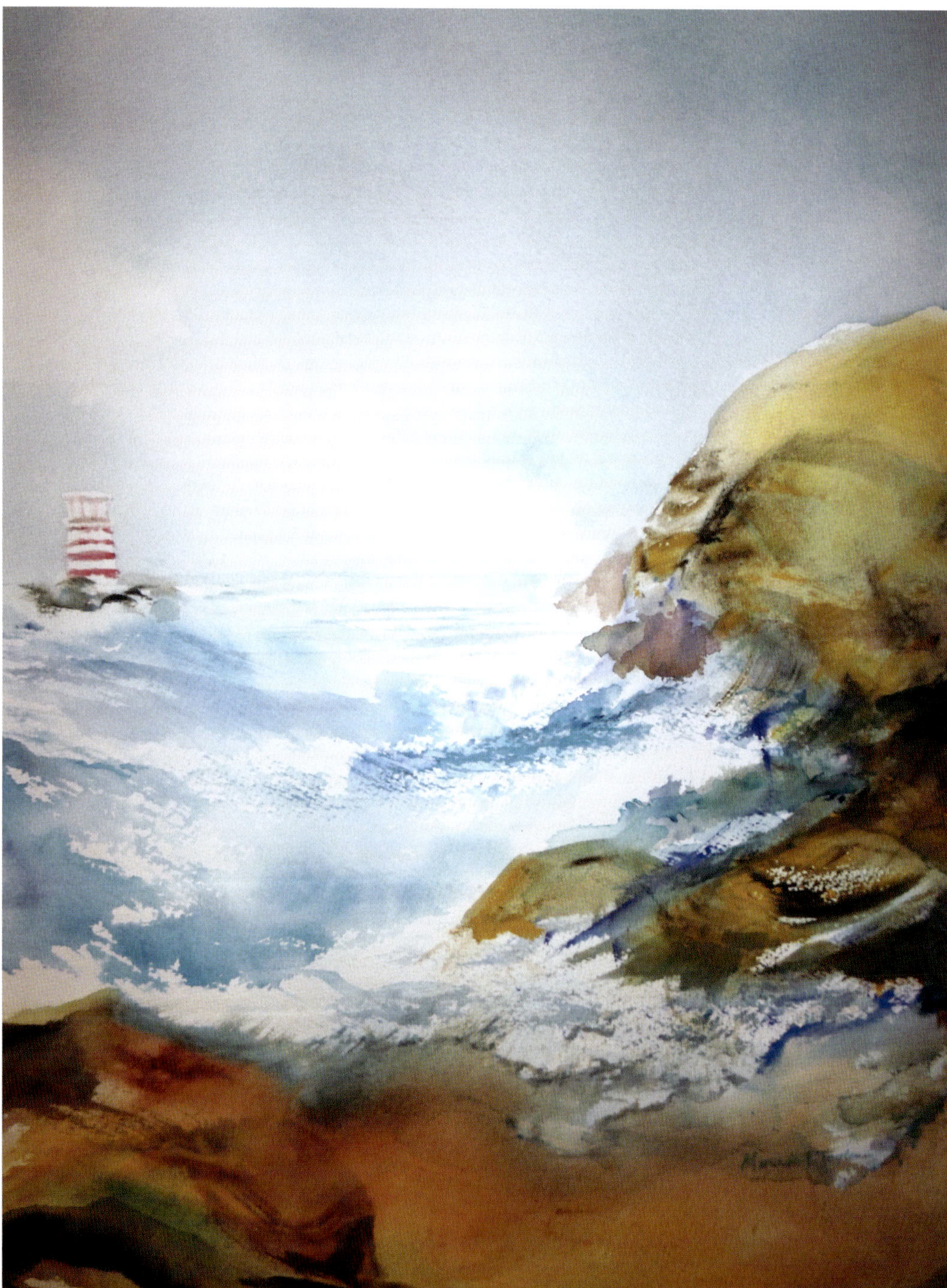

Land's End, San Francisco
16x12

THE DARK DAY, APRIL 19, 1978

While teaching my eight-thirty morning class at the university, I hear a knock on my studio door.

"Come to the phone now; there is an emergency." The secretary's eyes do not meet my glance as usual.

"Your wife is in the hospital; and your daughter, Lucy, too."

"What happened?"

"An auto crash," the secretary says. "They are at St. Joseph Memorial Hospital. Your family doctor, Wilfred Hechanova, is already there taking charge."

I jump into my workhorse car and head northwest on Highway 139 toward St. Joseph, Michigan. Halfway there, I see my wife's vehicle off the road, literally wrapped around a tree, the front end totally smashed.

I stop long enough to grab her blood-covered purse from the car. I leave Lucy's spa bag. I don't think my skull is strong enough to contain the explosion within my brain. I have to see them again. I breathe deeply and drive safely, praying all the way to the emergency room.

Within the hour a friend has taken the three other children from school and brought them to the hospital. The three boys, Leonard, Lowell and Lyndon, and I gather around their older sister, Lucy. Her bruised body is lying on a gurney in the emergency room. Obviously their sister's leg is broken in two places and needs to be set. I hug my kids tightly. We can hardly speak.

The boys and I decide to escape the frenetic atmosphere of the distressed patients and overworked doctors. We walk down the hall and find a quiet place in the St. Joseph Hospital Chapel. I pray out loud, "Creator God, please love Elaine as much as we do. Our teens and I need her. But if Mom's brain is dead, please let her body pass also."

The surgeons valiantly try from nine o'clock until mid afternoon to save my wife's life. They exhaust the total blood supply of the county. The hospital sends an ambulance for more blood from the Kalamazoo area. The doctors will not grant my request to visit Elaine, so I suspect the worst. My family doctor does not have the courage to tell me, but I sense that both her mind and body are now at rest. A surgeon, whom I have not met, breaks the news that my beloved wife and my children's mother has passed. Heroic measures have failed to keep her heart beating.

Lucy is partially sedated, but she groggily describes what happened. "I was in the front seat sitting next to mother. Mom was driving normally. With no warning whatever, a car careened toward us, in our lane, at high speed. This idiot came zooming over the hill passing in spite of a solid yellow line." Pausing to wipe a tear, Lucy continues. "To avoid a head on collision, Mom was forced off the road."

"That's enough," I say as I squeeze my daughter's hand.

Later that day I receive a call from a high school teacher in our town. He corroborates Lucy's story and adds, "I was right behind the reckless driver. There is no doubt in my mind that he knew what happened, but he just kept right on going."

The headline in *The Herald -Palladium* reads, "Police Seeking Car Following Woman's Death." The article continues, "M. Elaine Taylor, 54, an assistant professor of piano at Andrews University in Berrien Springs, died of injuries Wednesday about five hours after her car was reportedly run off the road and crashed into a tree."

Soon after Elaine dies, Lucy receives the care she needs. The doctors set her bones and put on a brace. When I visit Lucy in the hospital the next day, I ask, "Would you tell me some more about Mother's last moments?

"Dad, it's painful to think about," Lucy says. "Mom was brave. She prayed about each member of the family. Her last words were, 'You will have to pray now. I can't any longer.'"

These are my words, the heart plea of a grieving husband, which I write soon after the fatal accident:

A streak of blood red rims the eastern horizon
Ominous ocher clouds sullenly hover low
Blackness prevents the sun from penetrating that
April morning
Desolate Sabbath after sleepless night.
Another morning the ankle-high grass wet with dew
Would have welcomed a loving pair
Now I wander aimlessly alone
Suddenly thorn bushes surround me
I wail aloud
In all directions tangled
Sharp branches thwart my path.
Throw yourself into them
It can't hurt worse
Time passes painfully

A blood red streak divides night from day
Life from death

My wordless prayer penetrates heaven. In agony I grab a branch of a black raspberry bush that had escaped cultivation. It breaks. Though teary-eyed, I noticed the immature flower and leaf buds developing along the apparently dead cane.

No witness can attest, but in that moment I grasp the hand of God. Tomorrow is resurrection day. The Holy Scriptures say, "If we be dead in Christ, we believe that we shall also live with Him." Romans 6:8.

I walk back to the house, bathe, make breakfast and awaken the children. Around the table we talk of Easter coming next week and the hope of seeing Mother Elaine in heaven.

Desolate. Elaine has left my side. She will not be in her place at dinner tonight. Nor will I hug her before going to sleep. Our children have lost their mother. I am a widower. Alone.

Dr. Smoot, president of Andrews University, where Elaine and I are professors of music, comes to visit that night. Pastors from Pioneer Memorial Church comfort our family. Teachers and classmates surround my children. Neighbors bring so many dishes of food that after meals, we freeze TV dinners for the future. A thousand people, including relatives, colleagues, and students, attend the funeral. The New England Youth Orchestra, a group that the four Taylors have toured with across the United States and Europe, play their praise. The eulogies trumpet their homage. The clergy pray their blessing. The mourners cry. I'm still alone.

Right after dinner one evening, I answer the telephone. "Hello … who is this speaking?"

"Dr. Taylor," says the voice on the other end, "I'm Beth, Beth Grady, a student doing research at Andrews University. Are you the music professor?"

"Yes, how may I be helpful?"

"If you were another person in this world, who would you like to be?" she asks.

"I didn't expect that question. Well, I don't think there is anyone else that I want to be except myself," I say.

Beth presses the point. "There must be somebody. Tell me who you would like to be."

"I still have no answer for you. Wait a minute, maybe …"

"Yes," Beth eagerly presses her point. "Please tell me who it is."

"You see, my wife died in an auto accident a few months ago. It was not her fault. A car careened toward her in a no-passing lane and forced Elaine off the road into a tree. She died hours after."

"I'm so sorry," says the voice of the student. "How could that answer my question?"

"Maybe you cannot understand," I continue thoughtfully. "My four children need her much more than they need me. I would gladly trade places with her if I could."

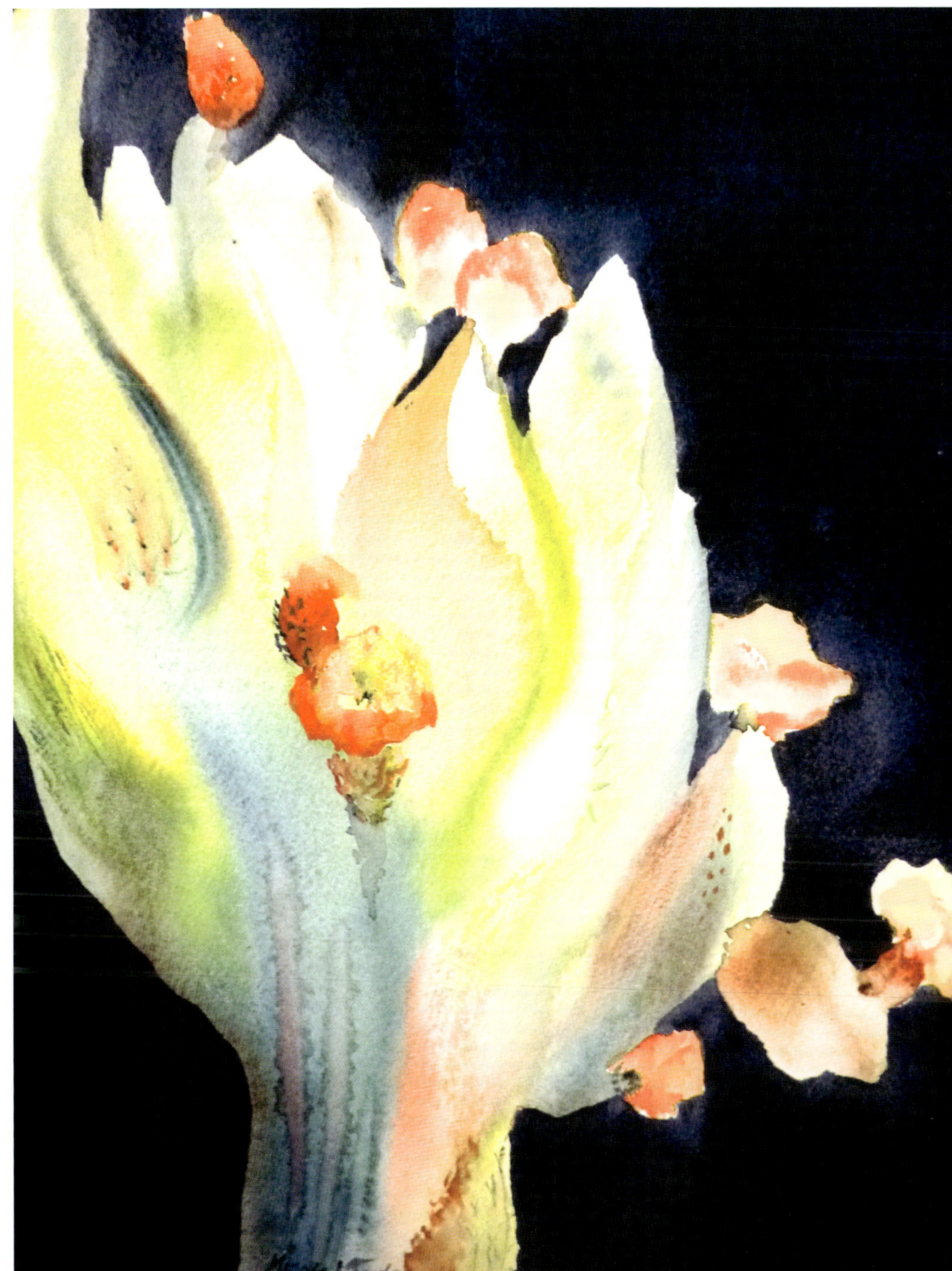

Beauty in Darkness,
12x9

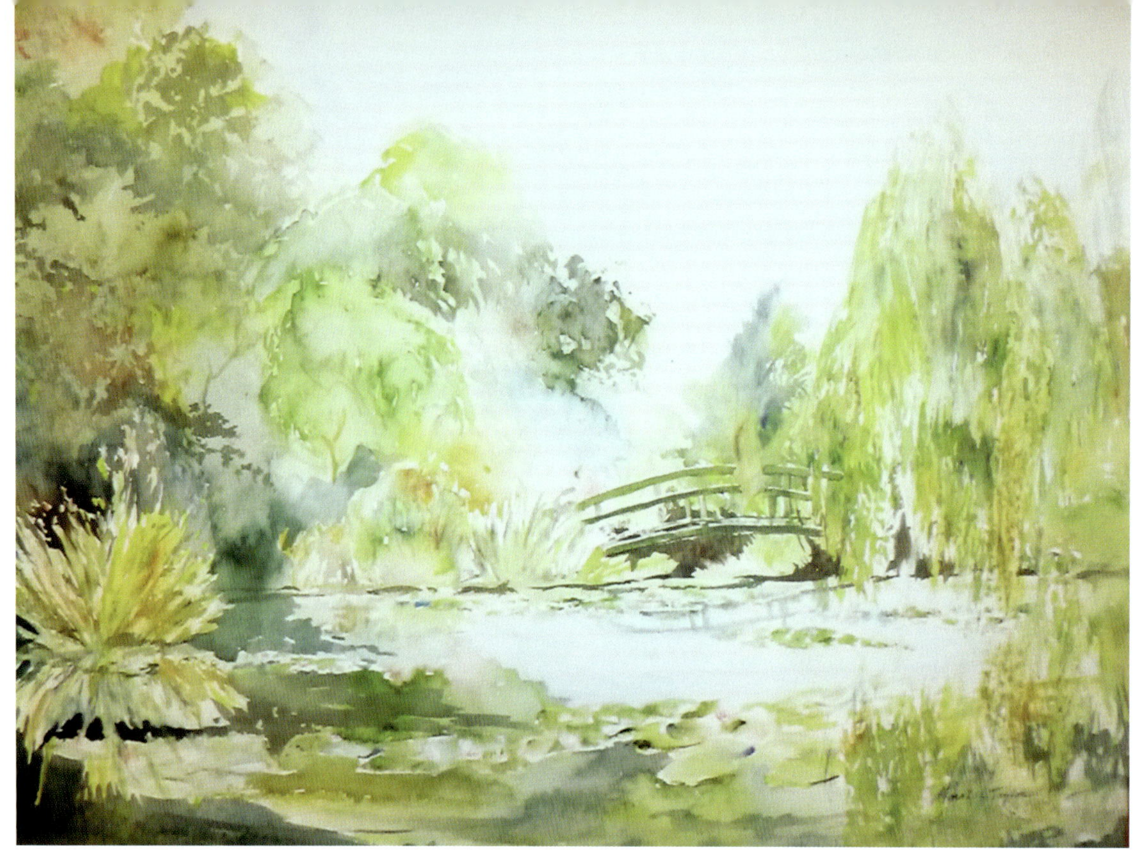

Monet's Garden in Rain, 16x20

MONET'S GARDEN

RAIN

Rain is a sculptor with chisel and hammer
    Pounding like thunder to carve palisades.
Rain is a veil iridescently shimmering,
    Flitting: It floats in capricious cascades.

Rain is a frantic and frenzied war goddess
    Swooping like eagle upon her huge prey.
Rain is a lover of bluet and columbine,
    Lulling, caressing his ladies each day.

Rain is a blare of intensive, harsh brass
    Beating its terrible rhythms in spite.
Rain is a velvety vapor, a mother
    Tucking her children in slumber for night.

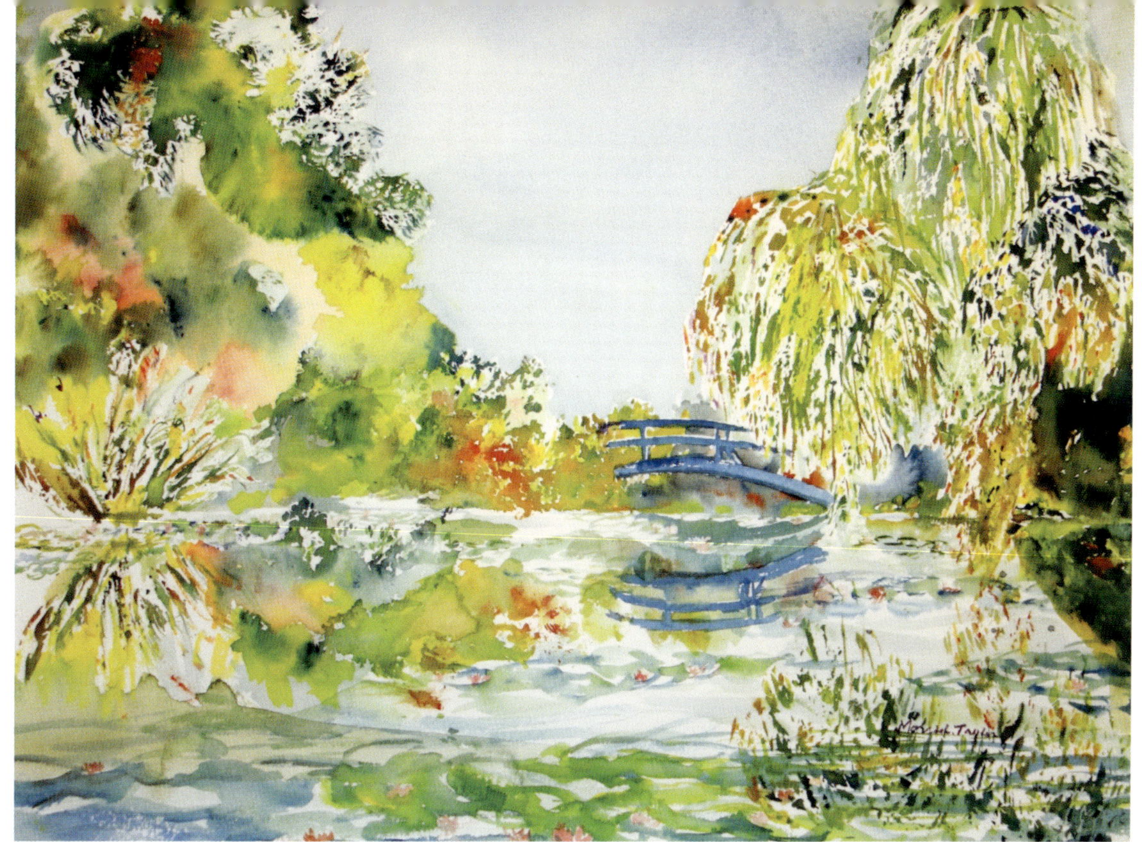

Monet's Garden in Sun, 16x20

SUN

Rose the sun today
   cowering soddenly
   drenched with rain
         Defy
         complain
Rose the sun today
   crouching sullenly
   the murky morning mist
         Unknown
         resist

Rose the sun today
   courageously
   cool clouds concealed the light
         Contest
         your plight
Rose the sun today
   dawning brilliantly
   daily orbit through morn
         A day
         is born

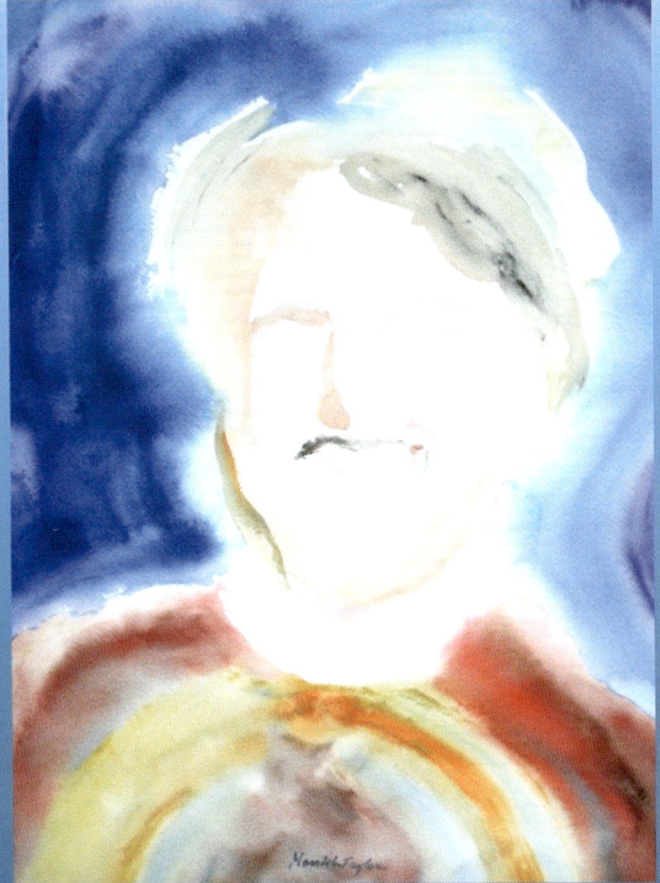

My Son Leonard Morris Taylor,
16 x 12 inches

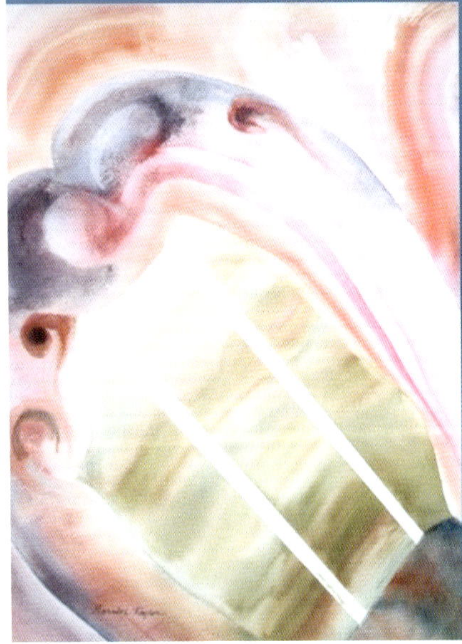

Depression Phase,
16 x 12 inches

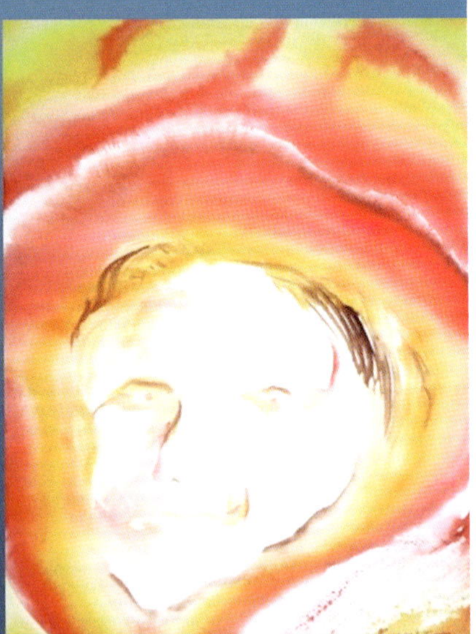

Manic Phase,
16 x 12 inches

ILLEGAL AMBULANCE RIDE

At nine in the morning I am teaching my graduate class in Baroque music. The telephone rings in my studio-classroom. The secretary in the music office has my schedule and knows that I should not be interrupted. I apologize to the class as I pick up the receiver.

"Is this Morris Taylor, Leonard's father?"

"Yes."

"I'm Dr. Glum, Leonard's psychiatrist. I advise you to forget that you have a son."

"Thank you for calling. I have been wanting for two weeks to have a conversation with you."

"I'm very busy," the doctor, replies.

"I'm teaching a class at the university right now. Can we make an appointment?"

"That will not be necessary. There is nothing to talk about."

"Maybe you could give me some ideas right now. What would you suggest?"

"I already told you. He's messed up. Just forget that you have a son."

"Sir, that is not possible …"

The doctor who is in charge of Leonard's case at the Berrien County Hospital hangs up on me.

Somehow I manage to regain my composure and finish the class. I reschedule my private piano lessons and classes for the rest of the day. I know that I have to get Leonard out of the clutches of this harmful psychiatrist whom I have never met.

I know about an outstanding medical director at the Seventh-day Adventist hospital in Battle Creek, Michigan. Through his mother, who had been my master's degree student in music, I make a direct contact with Dr. Schmidt who agrees to accept my son as a patient.

Later that day I succeed in contacting the legal services at the county courthouse.

"Sir, about two months ago my son, Leonard Taylor, tried to commit suicide three ways. Then he totaled his car around midnight by crashing it into an apple tree in blizzard conditions."

"Wait a minute," says the attorney. "How old is your boy?"

"He's a grown man of thirty," I continue. "He was admitted and treated at the county hospital in St. Joseph, Michigan. After his body mended sufficiently, he was transferred to the psychiatric unit where he has been under evaluation and treatment for a month. They have allowed almost no contact with me, his dad." Then I tell the county-employed lawyer about the phone exchange earlier that day.

The attorney says, "I don't blame you for seeking help elsewhere. I do not have the authority to order a transfer. No one can do that without a court order."

"What would happen if I could get him admitted to a better mental facility?"

"That is not easy. You not only need to have an acceptance, but you also have to find a way to get your son to voluntarily admit himself. The most you can hope for is a thirty-day restraining order. After that the matter has to go before a judge."

"Yes, I anticipated that scenario. The medical director in Battle Creek has already agreed to issue the restraining order and to accept him as a resident patient. From tales from his mother Dr. Schmidt already knows about Leonard's long term mental illness and his predilection to suicide."

The attorney leans closer. "Don't tell anyone. I think the only way you can get your son there is to hire an ambulance. You will be taking a chance, but once you cross the county line you will be legal. I will issue a statement for his discharge from the Berrien County hospital."

Before office closing hours that day I arrange for an ambulance to pick up my son the next morning. Even in 1988 dollars, the seventy-five-mile ride is expensive. I have in my possession official papers that will release Leonard from the hospital; I am unsure about the legality of his transfer to the ambulance.

The next morning I arrive on location at the same time as the ambulance and present the legal document. I look out the window of my car to see Leonard being ushered from the maximum-security unit into the waiting ambulance.

I follow the ambulance like an accident chaser. I drive with aggressive caution to keep up the pace. Once on Interstate 95, I fear that I am breaking the speed limit. I keep one eye on the road and another on the rearview mirror.

When I cross the county line, I think, *At least the illegal portion of the journey is over. Now all I have to worry about is a potential speeding ticket.*

With expert talk therapy and appropriate drug dosage Leonard improves over the month. According to law he must have an evaluation and a hearing in thirty days. The psychiatrist prescribes at least another month of hospitalization. Leonard refuses to sign the extension, so a formal legal hearing is mandated.

At ten o'clock on the appointed Tuesday, I show up at the courtroom. Leonard has chosen to represent himself rather that allowing the court-appointed attorney to speak for him. That means that I am cross-examined by my son. He asks, "Why do you, Morris Taylor, think that you know what is best for me? Do you think that I am crazy?"

"No, Leonard, I don't think you are crazy. I want you to take appropriate psychotropic medicines and to cooperate with the doctors who can make you well," I say.

"I know what is best for me. I'm not going to stay here any longer," he replies.

"That may not be your choice. I plan to accept the recommendation of the medical team," I counter. "I hope you will cooperate. It hurts me as much as it pains you, son."

I write a note for consideration by his psychiatric team: "At first Leonard's periods of depression seemed to come and go. To his family they appeared to be related to his drug and alcohol problems. Gradually his periods of depression deepened and came closer together. He became less functional at school or work. According to social security records his total earnings for a decade stand at about $3,000. The four suicide attempts confirm this trend.

"Several things about Leonard's present condition

alarm me. When I see him, I can tell that he has similar thoughts and feelings to those that preceded his most serious suicide attempt. His weight is at an all-time adult low. His integration with other persons is about nil; he is withdrawing, receding further into himself. His religious fixation seems to be more intense than ever, making it difficult to talk with him about any other thing."

I think to myself, *If this team cannot bring him back to some sort of reality, I fear that my son may never be a functional person again.*

The judge rules that Leonard should remain in treatment for another thirty to sixty days at the discretion of the mental health team. This extension gives him the necessary medical treatment to survive a while longer. Leonard's stepmother, Rilla, and I support every good therapy we can find. Sometimes Leonard stays in therapeutic institutions both public and private. At other times, his treatments take place within group homes or with friends. For a decade, the question is not if, but when, my son will leave us.

1991 proves to be a difficult year for Leonard. With the family's blessing Leonard enrolls in a church-related program designed to overcome his addiction to unprescribed drugs and to help him faithfully take the medicines prescribed by his psychiatrist. Hopefully, he can live on his own in a protected environment in Bowling Green, Kentucky, supporting himself with odd jobs at a music store and a carwash. Family members visit him on several occasions to encourage him. Despite the help of a medical doctor, an addictionolotogist and a psychotherapist, Leonard's mental state worsens. Sometimes he swallows his medicine; at other times he relies on prayer.

Local authorities forcibly admit Leonard to Western Kentucky State Hospital a number of times. Sometimes he is treated as a resident and at other times he requires restraints and forced medication. On the day that he is to have a legal trial, Leonard serves as his own lawyer, talks his way out of the hospital via a chaplain, and collects his back social security checks totaling several thousand dollars. I have seen this pattern many times over decades. Every person in our immediate family has invested resources of time and money in Leonard's recovery. Many kind people do their best to help. As his father, I often wonder what more or better I can do. Some nights I sleep fitfully, and many days I experience difficulty concentrating.

In late December of 1991, my son, Leonard, gives his dad a great gift. He comes home for the holidays. The whole family is thrilled to see Leonard. I am pleased to see him doing well, but I am inwardly apprehensive about his mental stability. I have a premonition that this might be the last chance to spend quality time with my oldest son.

Our house in Buchanan, Michigan, is situated on three acres of land between Red Bud Trail and the St. Joseph River. The great room has a huge Indiana sandstone fireplace that occupies the far wall and extends outdoors for fifteen feet. The wall that faces the river is completely double glass with air between for the extreme cold of winter and hot humidity of summer. From the glass wall the redwood ceiling slants upward, forming a clerestory of narrow glass windows facing south. The positioning of the windows gives complete privacy without curtains.

Christmas in our home brings fun. Rilla prepares healthful, home cooked meals. I enjoy splitting wood and gathering kindling for our cheery fires. Everyone in the family participates in music whether piano, stringed instruments or singing. Our Christmas tree this year is a twelve-foot fir extending to the tip of the cathedral ceiling. We make ornaments by folding paper and cutting patterns to make six-pointed stars that we cover with glue and glitter. We string the metallic tinsel strand by strand to imitate icicles.

Now Leonard is home. The Taylor String Quartet with Leonard as the first violin, Lyndon as second violin, Lucille as violist and Lowell as cellist, are practicing for church. I, the proud father, soak up the chamber music like old times. That evening I listen to a private concert. I absorb every nuance of the "Andante Cantabile" from a Tchaikovsky String Quartet. These are the last notes I hear my children play together as a string quartet.

The next day, Sunday, I drive Leonard to the Greyhound bus station in South Bend just over the border into Indiana. We talk pleasantly about the good times and his future. I particularly thank him for coming home and participating in the holiday activities even though I realize that this required an earnest effort on his part to live through his pain. He thanks me for a great vacation saying how good it was to be home again.

I board the bus with him. I lift his tattered suitcase into the overhead bin with presents I have placed inside. Rilla has packed a large lunch sack filled with nutritious food. I already have sent ahead a check for several months rent to Leonard's landlord. Inwardly, I am pained that I cannot trust my son with cash, since from previous experiences, I know that cash may be spent on drugs he does not need. We hug quickly as the driver is about to shut the door. As I wave toward Leonard's sad face in the bus window, I turn to cry privately. That is the last time I see my son alive.

On March 14, 1992, Leonard runs in front of a Ford Bronco truck near the Citrus Bowl Stadium in Orlando, Florida. A few days later I fly to Orlando to identify his body. Leonard lies in an improvised coffin at the city morgue. With horror in my eyes and a trembling in my voice I say aloud, "This is my beloved son, Leonard Morris Taylor. How I love him."

All the way back home I sob into a pillow I have brought with me. My son was handsome, intelligent, gifted—everything a father could desire. Out of the airplane window I discern a vast, unbounded eternity wafting my son away from me. I cannot even ask the questions for which there are no answers.

My own psyche changes. Am I not a homosexual like Leonard? Do I not suffer that inner disconnect between the way I live in public and long to live in private? Grief nearly overcomes me. I admit myself to a mental hospital to give me a chance to gain equilibrium, to sort through my grief and to deal with my own homosexuality.

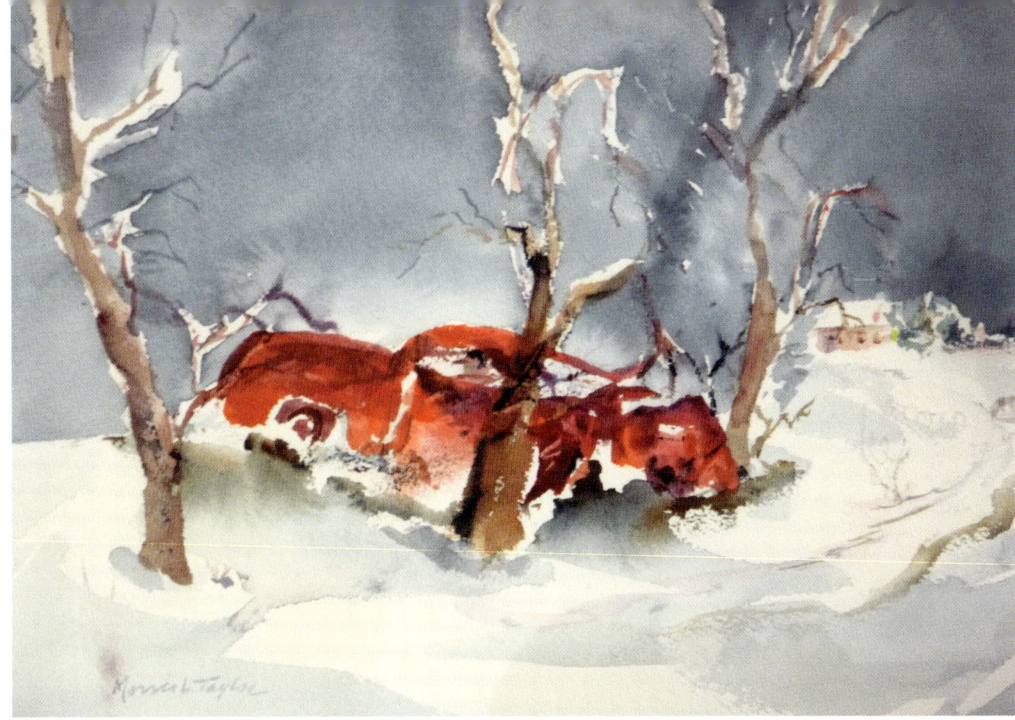

Mysterious illness overcomes you;
the battle rages within your mind.
Since your mother's fatal accident,
and often before,
death seems better than struggle.
A self-inflicted grave is yours.
Your life has vanished
like sand through a sieve.

Troubled by regrets,
I forgive your precipitous parting.
As by the stars birds migrate,
so we navigate as father and son.
Travel the universe
knowing a celestial Guide
keeps us in synchronicity.

Bon voyage, Leonard
I love you.

Leonard's Car Wreck
Grieving Father

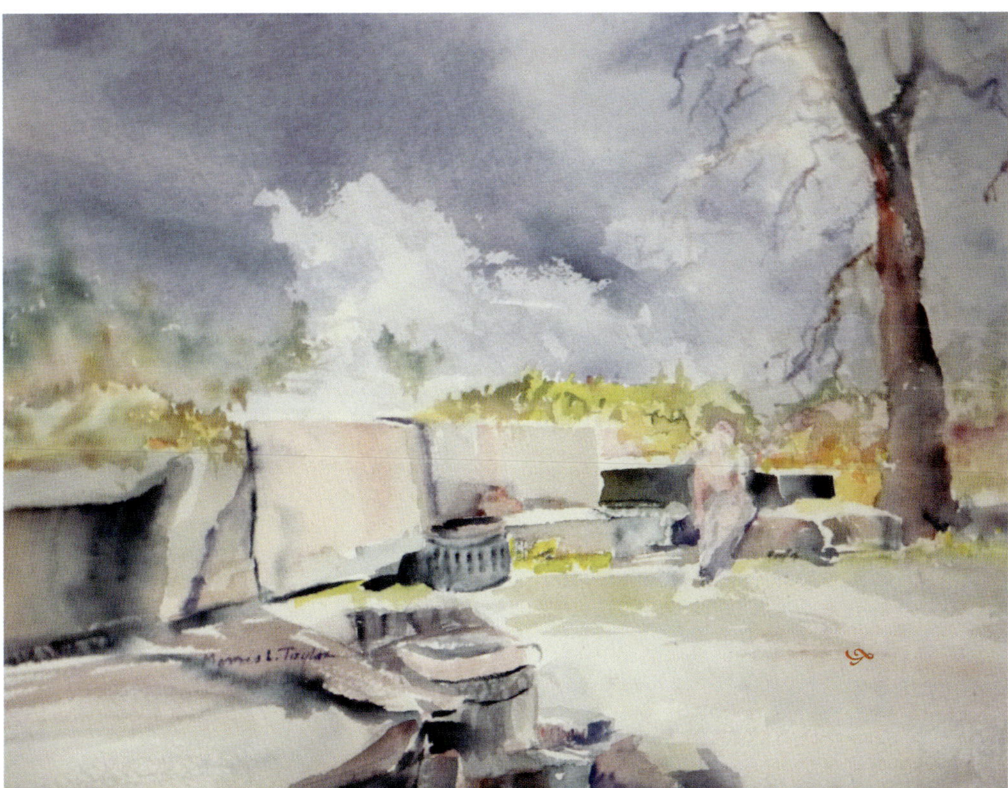

The Purple Torso, 16x12

SMOKE, MIRRORS, GO-GO-BOYS

I feel strangely attracted to the Lucky Horseshoe as I am alone in the big city on a cold and windy winter's night. I have never been inside a gay bar before. Well, any bar for that matter.

The brick building hugs the sidewalk on North Halstead Street, Chicago, the southern border of a section of town called by gay guys, "Boystown." Through the plate glass windows a passerby sees two red neon signs reading, "Lucky Horseshoe Lounge." A wooden door with chrome fittings invites you to enter. The interior walls of the bar are lined with mirrors lit by orange-red light fixtures in art deco style.

As I enter, my eyes sting from thick smoke. My throat is parched. I order cranberry juice with a lime in the glass. The bare chested bartender smiles and slides the drink down the well worn oak bar.

In the semi-darkness I can make out the form of a lithe body on a raised dais writhing in rhythm to thumping music. When I wipe my dripping nose, I smell liquor fumes mixed with the acrid sweat of shirtless men. Some are attractive, having kept their bodies in shape and their personalities bright; others are repulsive, slumped over their drinks, paying little attention to what's going on.

What are you doing here? Your guardian angel left you at the door, I think. I move back toward the entrance. Is this for a gulp of fresh air or to escape into the sub-zero night? Curiosity draws me back into the crowded bar.

Rather than stare, I steal glances into the wall-to-wall mirrors. A more masculine guy is now on a low stage. Strobe lights flash mini rainbows from sweaty rivulets on his muscular legs. Dollar bills are not the only bulge in his jock strap. He is horny enchantment personified.

Then I catch a glimpse of myself in the mirrors. My private tears help me cope with the smoky haze. My quiet sniffles betray my inner grief. I do not belong here. If anyone at my church-related university finds out, my career is history. I recall Magda in Gian Carlo Menotti's *The Consul* when she sings her desperate aria, "Is there anyone to whom the heart can be revealed?"

Just then a tall man with a starched clerical collar walks into this den of iniquity. Maybe I have company. *Perhaps he is someone who would care*, I tell myself. *No way*, I argue back. *He's probably like all the regulars who seem self-absorbed.*

The clergyman does not turn heads. No one kisses him or drapes their arms around him as they do other cute guys when they enter the bar. I figure that I'm on the path to hell anyway. I might as well sidle up and see if I can strike up a conversation. It's his fault for being here dressed like a man of the cloth.

I leave a chair between us, like I have read about in a book on gay etiquette. Then I lean over. "May I buy you a drink?"

"Yeah, okay," is the way I interpret his lip movement.

"What are you drinking?"

I order a beer for him and another juice for me. The chair between us is still empty, so I slide over so I can hear better.

We chat and exchange first names. This guy is for real. He is here to talk, kind of like helping guys cope with sexuality or depression. Gradually I feel more comfortable despite having to shout at close proximity into his ear, and he into mine.

The blaring music changes to a softer beat. In the mirror I see a go-go boy on the bar top, more my age and build. *He's cute. I could go home with him*, I think. My conscience argues, *Oh, no you don't. Even the thought is adulterous.*

"Uh, as I was saying, Reverend, I'm having a terrible struggle inside of me. You see, nobody knows. I've always been this way. Please help me figure out my sexuality in relationship to my religions beliefs."

"I understand more than you know," he responds. "Heard of Bob Jones University? I used to be an administrator there. One morning when I came to work, the president confronted me with some rumors. With no chance to defend myself or explain, he ordered me to clean out my desk and leave immediately. I was forbidden to talk to anyone. I lost everything. Completely banished and shunned."

My first reaction is horror. Quickly, I project this story upon myself. I have just told him my real first name, also the denomination of the church that sponsors my university. I even mention that I am into classical music and hate the eardrum destroying decibels around me.

What if he betrays me?

So here is the real mirror. I see myself in this administrator-turned-preacher. I confront the palpable threat of revealing anything to anyone, anywhere, anytime. I must remain a closeted homosexual living within the most strict parameters of secrecy. In two or three years I can retire at age sixty-five with my pension in tact.

I slip a Lucky Dollar into the shorts of the sexiest go-go dancer as I leave the Lucky Horse Shoe bar that night.

The next day I return to teaching at my fundamentalist university—one foot out of the closet, the other still firmly rooted inside.

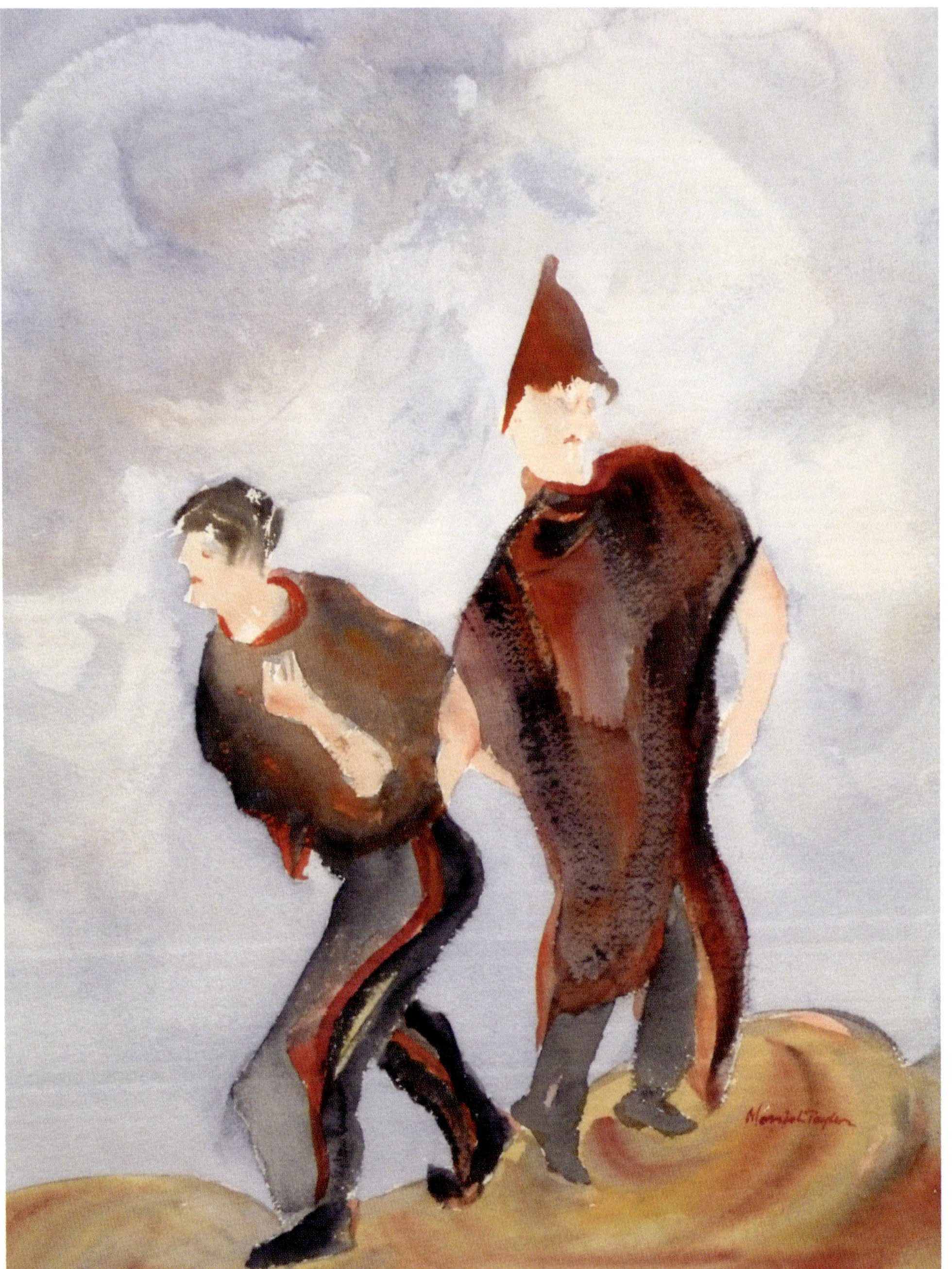

Parting Sorrow, 16x12

78

I LOVE AUCTIONS AND MEN

The pursuit of a masterpiece for the price of a reproduction suits me fine. *If you can't tell the difference between butter and margarine, you don't deserve the butter*, I tell myself.

At first I am chary of raising my hand, nodding my head or raising my paddle at auctions. Expendable income is in short supply while teaching on a missionary wage. I have four teenage children to educate. *If you don't have a specific use for the lot being auctioned, you don't really need it*, I admonish myself.

But oh, the thrill of the chase! Something like this Pendergast watercolor comes up so rarely at auction. Maybe just this once I can treat myself to acquiring a lovely painting. I do sneak in several bids in the hundred-dollar range before the bidding takes off into the thousands from the telephone buyers. *If you have no experience with this type of art, you are likely to accumulate a fake*, I warn myself.

A group of old quilts arrive on the auction block. My intuition tells me that this is a great bargain. There are so few of these handmade quilts in the wedding ring pattern, and since most people would want such exquisite needlework, I can sell merchandise and make money. *You do not know what this auction lot is worth on the market, and you have yet to identify a potential customer*, I scold myself.

In the neighboring town of Bridgman, Michigan, a genial old man organizes local consignments into a weekly auction. Most Tuesday evenings fifty to eighty locals gather to gossip and bid. More valuable things like a motor scooter, a hand-painted vase or an antique table are auctioned separately. Median value items of consequence are grouped into lots placed on tables improvised from sawhorses with planks on top. Other stuff is shoved into boxes under the tables or overflowing onto the lawn. This is fun. For a twenty-dollar bill I can pick an odd box lot, kind of like playing the nickel slot machine, no real gamble. *If you are storing this junk or intending to give it as a gift to someone someday, you shouldn't accumulate clutter and junk*, I think to myself.

One particularly memorable auction takes place on the Fourth of July. The auctioneer, Leslie Hindman, flies by helicopter from Chicago to a country estate near our home in southwest Michigan. Jeremy, the property owner, had died in the pursuit of the vision of eating his breakfast at the North Pole. His charter plane crashed en route. I know the guy because he had a booth in the same antique mall where I exhibit some of my wares for sale. Sedate male couples and the shirtless young men predominate in the audience, which confirms my suspicion that the late owner was a homosexual. The higher priced items sell first. The sun beats down on the crowd seated in the open air. I bid successfully on clustered lots that auction for increasingly low prices as the audience thins. In addition to a carload of quality antiques that I buy in the outdoor sale, I successfully bid on a whole dresser full of underclothes. *When I wear some of the exotic and sexy underwear, I feel close to this gay man*, I tell myself.

A few months later, I am in pursuit of larger treasure, so I drive two hours to Chicago. About once every two months I take a day off from teaching to observe John

Haenzel and his dad auction off quality consignments of estate merchandise. For nearly two years I just watch and evaluate. Then I cautiously enter the bidding wars.

One auction I am sitting in the front row when a Marc Chagall lithograph goes on the block. Bidding discretely by holding my paddle close to my knees, I hear, "Sold to the man at that end of the first row." I am both thrilled and remorseful. Six hundred dollars is more than I intend to spend. *Is it real? Who will buy it?*

Before I overcome the shock of my rash bid, the person sitting next to me gives me a nudge and hands me this note: *Do you want to sell the stone lithograph?*

I answer back in writing: I like the print of Abraham and Isaac; I intend to keep it, thank you.

Then I glance their direction and observe that the older lady is excitedly conversing with a younger woman that appears to be her daughter. Another note: *We own several Chagalls and we came here just to acquire this particular one. What is your price?*

I reluctantly, yet exultantly, reply: *Two bills.*

With no hesitation an envelope travels the well-worn route along the front row.

Two crackling hundred dollar bills accompany the next communication. I write a note to the auctioneer. "Reassign Lot Number 87. The buyers will pay the premium and also the sales tax."

For a decade after that I compete at the better estate auctions in the Midwest. My business, Arts and Antiques, flourishes. At the climax of my career I sell at Sunday shows thirty to forty times a year. I intend this to be my retirement business. I show merchandise in booths at nine malls in Michigan, Indiana and Illinois.

When I retire from the faculty of Andrews University at age sixty-five, I spend a year liquidating my thriving antique business. Although I receive status as Professor Emeritus of Music for my successful, forty-year career, there is no reason to keep living near the university. I am not invited to teach a favorite class, to attend faculty meetings or to enjoy social events. My homosexuality does not fit with church beliefs; therefore, my spiritual ministry as a Seventh-day Adventist has closed. As the news of my sexuality spreads, my colleagues, students and friends ignore me. I feel isolated and disconsolate.

At a weekend leather event near Philadelphia, I meet Tyler. We discover that we have many things in common: an interest in the leather scene, a love of classical music and a need for a roommate. Tyler invites me to live with him in his rent-controlled apartment on Nob Hill in San Francisco. He travels to Niles, Michigan, by train. We rent a U-Haul trailer and drive across the continent with a few possessions. My Steinway grand piano follows later via a professional mover.

In this new environment I flourish. I build a new life discovering new facets of Morris's personhood. Since I cannot play my piano often or teach lessons in the rent-controlled apartment, I develop as a watercolor artist, showing my art in thirty one-person shows over a period of twenty years. I feel comfortable accepting my homosexuality and the leather lifestyle in dress and behavior. When Tyler retires, he moves into a life-care facility. I build a new relationship with Jonathan. We purchase a condo in the Castro district of San Francisco where we live happily as a married couple. I no longer attend auctions to buy antiques. I do continue to love men.

MENTAL HOSPITAL FOR ME

On March 14, 1992, at about 2:30 am, my son, Leonard Morris Taylor, commits suicide by jumping in front of a Ford Bronco near the Florida Citrus Bowl, the iconic football stadium in Orlando, Florida. Two days later the police locate me at my home in Buchanan, Michigan, to tell me the news.

Almost immediately I make the journey by plane to the scene of his death. I have never been in a morgue before. It is sepulchrally plain and painfully clinical. Through a glass window I gaze into the open casket.

I blanche. My tongue swells. An uncontrollable palsy shakes my frame. As instructed, I identify his body. In a hoarse gasp I say, "This is my beloved son, Leonard Morris Taylor. How I love him." I am the father after whom he is named. I was present at his birth. I now claim his body.

How I wish that I could have prevented such a tragedy! I know that Leonard had problems with mental illness since his early teens. He subscribed to *Psychology Today* and self diagnosed his condition. His first brush with the law occurred when he tried to pass a fake prescription to get the help he needed. His life was adversely affected by the false attitudes of our Seventh-day Adventist religion toward four hot-button issues: mental illness, drugs, guilt and sex. Believing that these four issues arise from willful disobedience to God's immutable law leads a person to despair. Trusting in Divine Power and counseling with clergy does not solve the problems of depression, addiction, illness and homosexuality. I should have pushed back harder against the preposterous doctrines of the church.

Now I find myself in danger on some of these same fronts, excluding the illegal drug aspect. In my grief I feel that I have let my son down. I might have set a better example or fought back more vigorously the dangerous misconceptions of religion. Maybe better therapy or another psychiatrist or a wonder drug might have saved him. Try as I did for two decades to find him professional help with appropriate medication, I still feel abject guilt. I know that I am a homosexual just as much as he was; only I have chosen to hide my homosexuality in a closet with seven doors in order to save my professorship at a Seventh-day Adventist university, which supports my family.

On September 27, 1994, I decide that I need psychiatric help for myself, or else I will erupt like a self-destructive volcano. I spend all morning telephoning each of the six mental hospitals that are on the approved list of Andrew University's insurance plan. I am ready to tell my second wife, Rilla, that I am going to voluntarily admit myself for psychiatric treatment the following day.

With the windows of my car rolled down I wait on campus behind the music building for Rilla to join me for lunch at the nearby school cafeteria. Along comes my senior pastor. He asks if he may join me. He is one of the few people who know that I am having difficulty coping with my son's death, and I think that a conversation with him might be helpful. I invite him to sit in the passenger's seat of my vehicle.

"Morris, how are things?"

"Sir, not really very good, but I am trying my best."

"We're here for you."

"I appreciate that. You know that my son and I are more alike than …"

"What about the adult Sabbath School class?" he interrupts. "Don't you think that this is a bit dissonant for you?"

I am shocked. "I have taught a Bible class for youth or adults all my life. This is my joy. My popular class meets in the choir loft and is broadcast throughout the campus," I respond.

I take the pastor's feigned concern as a thinly veiled threat to me stemming from his incomplete and prejudicial knowledge about my homosexuality. I point to the passenger seat where he is sitting. "Sir, if Jesus were sitting where you are, He would say, 'I love you.'"

That is more than he can tolerate. He has no words of comfort or acceptance. I cannot share with him anymore. That is when Rilla appears. She and the preacher exchange some pleasant conversation that I do not recall.

The next day I drive with Rilla to a secluded hospital in Allegan, Michigan. The fact that they have a lesbian on staff is one of the deciding factors in choosing this setting for my therapy. When the one small suitcase I bring is searched and my shaving equipment is removed, I discern that nobody here trusts me. Halfway through a nearly sleepless night, I get up for the toilet. Eerily, I realize that I am on suicide watch, alone, with locked doors and observation windows. I am not sick, yet I want to die.

At breakfast consisting of tired fruit, packaged cereal and greasy pastries served on paper plates and plastic utensils, I am informed that I have an appointment with a counselor at ten that morning. My "gaydar" is out. I am quite sure this gal is that lesbian whom the admitting officer had told me about on the phone the day before. My suspicions are verified in the chit-chat about her arrival at work that morning on a Harley Davidson motorcycle.

Then out of the blue comes the question, "How did you plan to do it?"

"Do what?" I say, feigning surprise.

"You know what I am talking about. How did you plan to do it?"

In the ensuing pause I think, *You're here to get well. Be honest.*

"I am driving my Chevy Suburban loaded with antiques," I confess. "This huge trailer truck is coming in the opposite lane. No houses, no witnesses. The driver would be safe, and I would be out of my misery."

"Did you actually intend to do this?" she asks.

"I had the chance. I almost did. At the last moment I chickened out."

Silence.

I tear up and bury my head. I certainly have never told anyone about this close encounter with death.

"Do you think that would be the end of the story?"

"Well, no. But I kind of wish it had been."

"What about the truck driver? I have a brother who runs these big rigs long distance."

My head reels from the grief of my son's death. Had

I not gone to the police station to reassure the truck driver who ran over him that I held no grudge? Of course, I did. "Honest, Ma'am, I just don't know anymore."

"That's why you are here in the hospital, and why we are having this conversation. You have to face the truth about yourself."

"I feel so exhausted."

"Would you like to talk with a priest or minister? Do you have a church connection?"

"Yeah, I do. I mean; I don't want to talk to anyone I know."

"What about someone from MCC, the Metropolitan Community Church? The pastor from Grand Rapids sometimes comes over to talk with lesbian, gay and bi-sexual patients."

"What is this community church? And how did you know I am gay?"

"You've got a lot to learn. I'll ask him to come over tomorrow, if that's all right with you."

"My pastor doesn't understand, and that pisses me off."

Early the next day, during the long conversation with the accepting MCC pastor, the pressure between religion and homosexuality begins to ease. I begin to figure out that I can be accepted as a child of God without having to adhere to or accept the obstacles placed between my heavenly Parent and me. I must bide my time. I will find my freedom.

On the first Friday evening of my residence in the mental facility, my wife, Rilla, visits me. The conversation is strained. She wants me to get better soon, and I want to be left alone to sort out my depression. She cannot fathom why I am having such a struggle with my homosexuality, and I cannot express why the moral teachings of our church give me such pain. She finds it difficult to think that I am heading for a life of self-destruction that will lead away from my heavenly destiny. And I find it difficult to live with a person who believes that I am going to hell if I insist on giving way to my gay sexual desires.

Group and individual counseling seems to help. My personal work involving counseling with therapists, analyzing my motivation and controlling negative emotions seems paramount to healing. I write seemingly endless outlines. In one labeled "Go," I look into the possible tragedies ahead. They include sexually transmitted diseases like syphilis and HIV/AIDS, a meaningless and lonely life ostracized from church and society, and maybe life as a mentally ill person prone to suicide. In one labeled, "Stop," I look into the possible obverse tragedies. They include a life of denial and repression of all sex, a dull and listless existence as a religious hypocrite, and rigid conformity to the expectations of society.

A bedrock question for me is, *Does God love me, a homosexual man, just as I am?* In my notes I write by hand: "I want desperately to believe, 'Yes.' I have yet to find a Biblical basis for condemning homosexuality as sin. God will not predestine a person to a state of homosexuality beyond his love."

For nearly three weeks I remain in the hospital, gaining my mental equilibrium. I feel queasy about putting anti-depressant drugs like Welbutrin and Zoloft into my body; however, I can't seem to cope without them. I write daily mood logs in which I describe any upsetting event, plus the negative emotions thus engendered, by working through the thoughts in three stages: Automatic Thoughts, Distortions and Rational Responses. I attend group therapy sessions to express my issues aloud and to empathize with others having similar problems.

In my distress and illness I actually resign my faculty position at Andrews University. Fortunately, I realize the mistake quickly, and I bring this to the attention of my psychiatrist. My behavior is linked to the situational depression stemming from my son's suicide. Dr. John Courtney, Psy D, a neuropsychologist, determines that my prognosis is good for the long term, and he volunteers to write a letter on behalf of my restoration to the faculty. The president, the dean and the department chair agree to reinstate my tenured position as a Professor of Music. When I retire a few years later, I achieve Professor Emeritus status.

Sometimes depression almost gains supremacy. Healing is hard work and comes slowly. Gradually the optimistic periods are longer than the pessimistic times. Finally, I am able to grab hold of my own inner strength to weather the present maelstrom and to survive no matter what the cost. That price may include leaving my church, my professorship and even my wife. I deserve to live.

I write this poem while I am in the mental hospital.

What a drag to be a fag!
I don't know where best to go.
Who will care if I'm not there
playing harps or using sharps?

Folks just stare; don't seem to care.
"You're no good. Do what you should!"
Why do Christians and musicians
say they love, yet stand above?

Can you say because I'm gay
you'll keep score; God loves you more?
I cannot budge; He is the judge.
My Lord tells me, "He will hold me."

I engage in holy rage.
Wish me well, or go to hell.
I'll forgive; we all can live.
I'm here to stay, and I am gay.

LATEX CATSUIT

Late in the evening I wander the streets of West Hollywood. The neighborhood seems vaguely familiar, like the one known among gays as "Boystown," the Halstead District of Chicago. A few carryout food shops remain open. Bars tout their drink and entertainment specials. Sex shops attract a few stray clients. No one knows I am here. I crave something exciting and different.

A dingy shop beckons me. I am embarrassed by the obvious sexual nature of the wares. A "Drastic Reduction" sign leads me deeper into its dark recesses. In a nonchalant swagger I walk past porno flicks, scanty underwear and penetration toys.

In a back room I peer into a bin of disheveled items placed on the floor. I fondle the mysterious black fabric that slinks from its glassine enclosure. It feels smooth, clammy and ever so sensual. I cannot resist rubbing the latex over my skin. I imagine how that ebony shroud will slink over my chest and nipples. I crave being encased in the rubbery jock. Is this a kink that I will truly enjoy?

The complete bodysuit seems to be my size. It's a good thing that I do not try on the super-tight suit. If I make one slight tear, I own the sexy garment. I do not know that talcum powder helps the latex glide over oily skin.

Should I take a chance on buying the gear of my fetish dreams? I wonder. My right hand slips into my pants pocket. I discover enough crumpled bills there to pay the deeply discounted price.

Before I plunk down my precious stash, I phone my

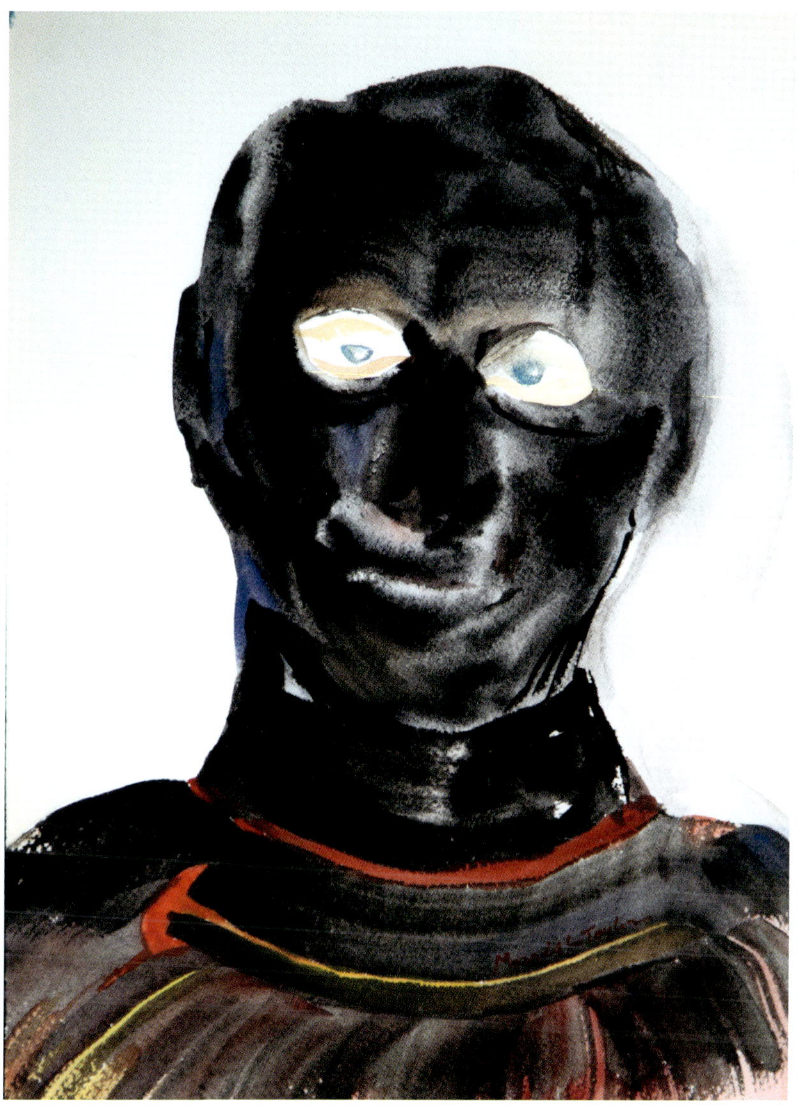

Rubber Paradise, 12x9

friend Mr. R, in Chicago. He is the founder and leader of Mister Rubber. "Thumbs up!" he says.

Now I own this weird outer skin. How can I, as a closeted homosexual, find a compatriot and playmate into rubber that will encase me in this desirably dreaded imprisonment? Maybe a guy in a leather bar or sadomasochism party will know somebody into rubber play.

One lucky night the glint of shiny latex suggestively dangling from my gym bag is enough to reveal my inner desire. An acquaintance secretly arranges a kidnapping. Against my conscious will, I am imprisoned and carried away into the land of my unconscious desire.

Several guys struggle for nearly two hours to slither my body into the neck entry of the catsuit. They use a huge can of talcum powder to help glide the black fabric over my skin. The shiny black catsuit tightly cradles every cranny of my anatomy, even individual fingers.

I am mummified in the tight, tomb-like garment. There are no holes in the snake-like garment except for tiny punctures for each nostril. I can hardly breathe in the taut, tight enclosure.

Where are my reliable senses when I need them? My vision turns as black as the latex of the suit. My hearing becomes eerily distorted. Though I can hardly swallow, my tongue tastes the acrid, rubbery material. With sight, smell and hearing curtailed, the sense of touch is exaggerated in response to temperature, pressure and irritation.

"Let's put him on a pedestal," says a guy with a vaguely familiar voice.

No, not with my acrophobia, I scream to myself.

An upward thrust. I'm being elevated onto some higher place. In vain I reach toward something to steady my balance. No sightline help to keep my body upright. Even the hands that placed me there are withdrawn. As a disembodied being, I float in space.

Time stands still. After a long period of tantalizing play, the fear of my tingling fingers and sheer exhaustion lead me to groan aloud. Anonymous persecutors patiently peel away the thin ply of latex. My sweaty, smelly body is finally released from its dank prison. My mind takes longer to return. My psyche remains in the never-never-land of space unfettered from volition and control.

Maybe my captor is the guy from Chicago? I think he has a vested interest. As my eyes adjust to the brightness, I rush to worship the man with whom I have bonded. "Rich, you rascal," I exclaim, "I should have known it was you."

Hey, I have the picture to prove all of this. In Rubber Pipeline, No. 1 of Vol. 2, there is a thumbnail with the caption, "MORRIS of Indiana models his catsuit for the MR [Men of Rubber] crowd."

I love my rubber catsuit. From time to time the garment has brought me much pleasure. The final act comes when a rubber top gets so passionate about my body in a catsuit that he becomes rougher than the aging man, I mean, rougher than the old garment, can endure.

Oh, the inexplicable joy of bondage: feeling inescapably confined, experiencing sensory deprivation, giving up control to the will of another, and being stimulated sensually and sexually.

That's paradise.

911 FOR AUNT RUTH ANN

No one is there to help that night. Neither my Aunt Ruth Ann nor her husband, Elton, manage to crawl to the phone. Elton falls in the bathroom soon after midnight. He is hard of hearing, and he is almost blind. His degenerative Parkinson's disease weakens his muscular control and affects his sense of balance. My aunt tries to pick him up from the floor. She then stumbles and breaks both legs. Two and a half days later a friend forces his way into their home. No food, no water, no medicine. It takes several hours to extricate the badly injured couple and to transport them to the hospital. A couple of months later, I fly from California to Massachusetts to spend ten days with my relatives in the long-term care facility. I first go to see my aunt. She is propped up in bed surrounded by faded flowers, overripe fruit and other useless stuff. In her condition I can't imagine how she can go home, and I don't know how to help her store or get rid of her possessions.

The hospital table is crammed with the makings of Bible verse cards. Ruth Ann carefully assembles these from used greeting cards with pinking shears, Elmer's glue and multi-colored glitter.

"I'm hoping the doctor will let me go back to our place on Shirley Road," she says.

"You're in no condition to take care of yourself alone," I advise.

A tear accumulates in one blue eye and falls down her cheek. "Yeah, you're right. I'm on a waiting list for an assisted living place."

"What about Elton?" I ask. "When I was in his room, I noticed that he can't walk or care for himself. It's so sad."

"Morris, I guess we're better off right here. At least I can get out of bed and roll in my wheelchair to his room." Ruth Ann is fat as ever, no, even more so. I think she must weigh over four hundred pounds. She has a special board on which her body slides from the bed into the wheelchair. It takes two nurses to even get her out of bed.

"Morris, you've not been listening," Ruth Ann interrupts my reverie. "I'm hoping the doctor's will let Elton and me go back to our place on Shirley Road." Then she adds, "Check on my cat."

"Where is Poopsabella?" I ask, remembering the huge tiger-striped monster my aunt usually held to her ample bosom. "Cross my heart; I'll see that he is okay. Your cat is better off in familiar surroundings."

The next day I visit Ruth and Elton's house. An industrial sized dumpster occupies almost the entire driveway of their clapboard New England bungalow. Judging from the overgrown grass and unkempt window boxes, the property is abandoned. Dare I open the front door? Had not Ruth Ann given me the key when I visited her in the nursing home? Now I remember the warning, "Morris, you may have to use the back door. The place is a mess."

I insert the key and finally get the rusty lock to yield. My head turns to avoid the horrible smell. Only the scurrying of creatures whose lair is being disturbed breaks the eerie silence.

With considerable effort I climb through the debris and succeed in opening a couple of windows. Then I flee to the outdoors for a breath of air. There is no way that I can get to the toilet, so I sneak out back to find relief amidst the white pines and overgrown weeds.

The enormity of my task begins to sink in. I must plow through. There is no other way that there will be enough resources to pay for their care. *Would she do it for me?* I wonder before a wave of guilt rolls over me.

I need help. Fortunately a few friends have gathered on the lawn. No time for niceties. I mobilize a brigade saying, "By seven o'clock tomorrow morning I expect quantities of large trash bags, heavy duty cleaning supplies and protective gear." These loyal people reach out by adding fresh water, plain food and good wishes. However, not one person volunteers to actually touch the junk or clean the filth.

I tackle the job on the first day. Fly specks dot all surfaces. Roaches flee every time I open a cupboard door. Unsealed containers are covered in slime. I fill dozens of plastic bags, carry them down the stairs, and throw them over the six-foot sides of the dumpster. By nightfall, I am exhausted.

And on the second day I realize that I have hardly emptied the kitchen. I manage to get some clean boxes and packing material for a few treasures like handmade linens from three generations. *What can I do with that cabinet full of salt and pepper shakers? Should I let anyone who comes near take his or her choice?* I mumble to myself.

When the friends come to bring lunch, I bark orders. "Early tomorrow go to Leominster and get some idle workers to help me lug trash. Buy ads in the local papers for a huge estate sale this Sunday. I don't care if it is the Fourth of July week. You've got find a way to get a second dumpster here tomorrow." My voice quavers. My eyes glaze over. "That's the least you can do," I say. "I've lugged my shoulders right out of their sockets."

On the third day I reach the front door. I suspect, correctly, that my overweight aunt is diabetic. Even through the gloves I get stuck with the sharps lurking in the couch cushions. *And to think that she was a nurse!* I fume. *She is just like her mother, only worse.* My muscles shake involuntarily from fatigue as I collapse into the only chair clean enough to sit on.

On the fourth day, I discover that the door to the second bedroom has not been opened since Ruth Ann's mother died many years before. I slash my way through spider webs that are nearly solid from floor to ceiling. One bureau contains Avon products in original boxes and tins. One of Ruth's supposed friend tries to steal them when I'm not looking. I arrange for their return. They will have value at the garage sale as collectors' items. The first overflowing dumpster is carried away.

And on the fifth day, I enter the basement. I give some usable items to curious neighbors in exchange for their help. I clear the garage out and make it the repository of a few things precious to save in case my aunt can move to assisted living quarters. Even though the hired help falter and quit, I tough my way through, working until darkness conceals the carnage.

By the end of Friday I have cleaned and priced most of the stuff for the yard sale. The second dumpster is full. My back aches. Just before sundown, the beginning of the Sabbath, I retreat to my bed and breakfast and go to sleep for ten hours. Breakfast Sabbath morning is leisurely. I choose not to attend church but rather take a two-mile, circular walk past old haunts.

I remember my Grandfather Freiberger as I pass the rustic cemetery where he is buried. I find the evergreen grove where I used to go on solitary picnics and the roadside ditches where the pussywillows heralded spring. A neighbor's barnyard looks just like it did when I first saw their ring-nosed bull mount a heifer. The village dump has been closed and bulldozed over; I used to call it "The Gold Mine" because I found so many treasures there. Most poignant all, I linger around the three acres my folks used to own. My unheated room was half of the front porch. I knew it was cold when the chamber pot froze under the bed. Alternately I rejoice or mourn memories. I bury some of them.

On Monday I visit Ruth Ann in the hospital for the last time; by then Elton had passed.

"The yard sale went well," I say. "You will have a check for at least two thousand dollars. I gave some of things that didn't sell to your friends. They all promised you can have your treasures back when you go home."

"Did you save out my dishes, and what about my dear Poopsabella?"

"Don't worry. The neighbors across the street have taken a liking to your cat; Poopsabella is safe. Margie has the best things in storage at her house. I couldn't leave things on the property to get stolen."

"I may never leave this rest home," says Ruth Ann. Pointing out the window to the nearby hospital she adds, "I've been over there three times now, each time for something different. I guess I just eat too much."

"Someday you'll have a nice place again, even if it is assisted living," I assure her.

When I look about the room, I see unfinished meals and lots of sweets. In my heart I know she will be very fortunate if she ever goes home. With her morbid obesity and lack of self-control, it will never be safe for her to live alone.

Ruth Ann's eyes tear up. "The only time I have been out of this old folks home was to attend Elton's funeral," she says. "Thanks for all you've done for me."

At this moment I tell myself, *Yes, I really do care, and I am a good person*. I regret all of this, but I can't bring myself to say how I remember how she took advantage of her husband and really abused him. *I guess they were good for each other in a strange sort of way*. "It wasn't much. You would do it for me," I say aloud.

Seething inside, I think. Why did you leave me this horrible mess? I'm exhausted. I hope that I don't get terribly sick from the dirty job.

I do manage a smile and give my aunt a hug around her spongy shoulders. To myself I say, *Ruth Ann, your conniving friends got the valuable New England property at the height of a boom. You left me a few crumbs, but I had to beg for them.*

"I did take some pictures and enough linens to wrap a couple of pieces of carnival glass," I tell her.

"I hope you didn't get rid of my stuff," she objects. "I'm hoping to get out of this place, you know me: I have to have my things."

Ruth Ann dies in the convalescent home a few months later. She can't take her possessions with her this time.

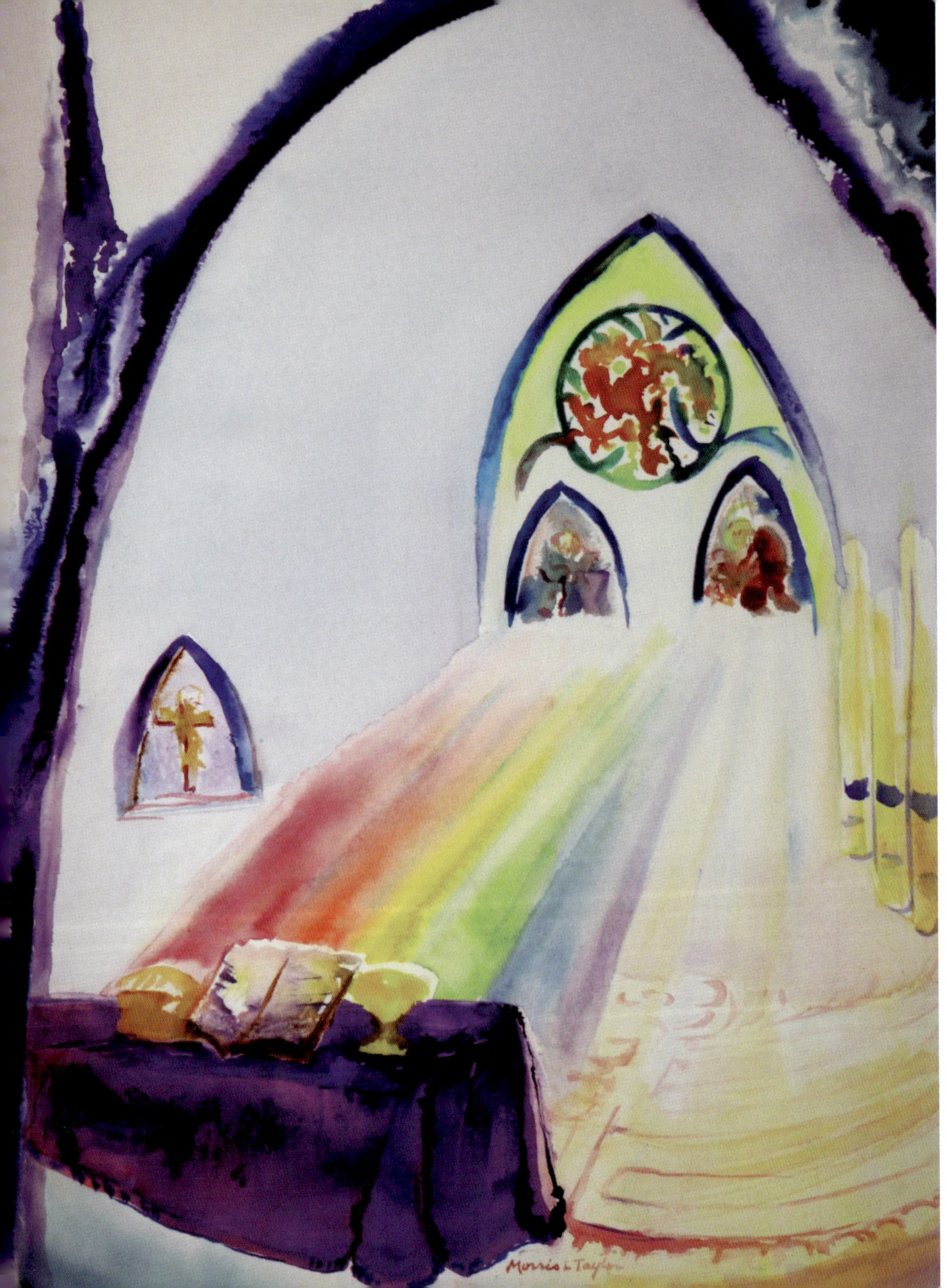

A HOUSE OF PRAYER FOR ALL PEOPLE

Sunshine Rainbow, 20 x 16

CHURCH OUTING
NO PICNIC

At a meeting of the Association of Adventist Forums I out myself to a church group for the first time. I feel proud that, at age seventy, I can tell my story in a public space. I reflect humbly on my life from the perspective of retirement, mortality and sexuality. I am ashamed of the years when I might have influenced the Seventh-day Adventist Church to be more tolerant of lesbian, gay, bisexual and transgender people.

One foggy day I am sitting at the reception desk in the nave of Grace Episcopal Cathedral. I greet guests from many countries and hand out welcome brochures in a dozen languages. With committee help I have designed "The Episcopal Church Welcomes Us" printed with a rainbow logo. These brochures help GLBT people feel at home in the cathedral. I also give a half-hour lecture tour explaining the adaptation of the Gothic architecture for earthquake prone San Francisco. This particular day I am chatting with visiting guests on the front steps of the cathedral. I discern that some of them are Adventists attending a theological conference in town.

That afternoon, while I am waiting at a traffic light to cross the intersection on the side of the five-star Fairmont Hotel, I introduce myself to a friendly looking guy, and we chat amiably. Come to find out, he is an Adventist pastor whose gay brother committed suicide. I am a former Adventist professor whose gay son committed suicide. We cry together right there on the street corner. One clergyman and one professor in synch no matter what their colleagues think.

A few months later my street corner friend, David Larson, DMin, PhD, writes me an e-mail. "Would you be interested in doing a joint presentation at the Adventist Forum? The suggested title is: 'Christianity and Homosexuality: Ethical Concerns.'"

I respond immediately. "Certainly. Share with me the details."

On October 12, 2001, Jim Kaatz, the leader of the San Diego Chapter of Association of Adventist Forums, meets me at the airport. He becomes my genial host for the weekend. I discover that he is the father of a professional cellist I know. That morning in church he introduces me and invites the congregation to a potluck and meeting. I give a brief testimony and play a piano solo.

The tension is palpable at the communal potluck. Smiles, handshakes and a few hugs, but mostly curious stares greet me. I think to myself, *Am I a gay clown beckoning for a sideshow or maybe one of the freaks inside? I've got to go through with this now that the circus is on the road.*

Dr. Larson and I sit on a raised platform facing the packed auditorium. After a few nice words of introduction, it is my turn to speak. I bring up the phlegm in my throat; it tastes like stomach acid.

"Hi! Many of you may feel conflicted or uncomfortable for whatever reason. I embrace your hurt and care about how you feel. We are in this together. Each person engaged in this discussion deserves our respect, regardless of whether others agree or disagree. So let's relax. We can be family."

Those are the formal words I have written down. My knocking knees and throbbing heart disagree. *It is possible to be both spiritual and gay? Just say it, Morris.*

Back to the script, "In your kind introduction, Jim, you mention that I am a Professor Emeritus at Andrews University. 'E' means 'out of' and 'merit' means that I deserve it.' My participation in this symposium in no way reflects the view of Andrews University. I am a homosexual person. It takes courage to tell you part of my story in a public setting. I did not choose to be gay. Given our lot within the church and society, no one I know would choose this sexual orientation. This is just who we gay people are and who I am."

I think to myself, *Phew. I'm proud of you, Morris. You just came out! The pillars of the church may fall like they did when blind Samson pulled down the columns of the pagan temple, but look around you. This building is not falling on your head.*

I continue to half-read, half improvise. "This is a summary of how things were earlier in my life. My proverbial homosexual closet had locked doors most of which I myself did not dare open. Silence and secrecy seemed the only safe haven; however, I feel cowardly for choosing this path. Yes, I have been married to two great women, and I have four wonderful adult children. Cultural deprivation and church condemnation kept me from any knowledge that would have been of help to me on my sexual journey."

I decide right there on the platform to confess what it feels like to be in a homosexual closet. *Go ahead, Morris. Risk it. Read the poem you wrote when you were contemplating coming out.*

COLOR ME GRAY
An opaque shadow furtively creeping along a wall
whose psyche is seldom seen.
A silver fox slinking across a wintry landscape
whose path is rarely traced.

COLOR ME GRAY
An old garment with color waning
by wearing and washing and wearing again.
Bright ideas mixing together to become
dulled and dingy in hue.

COLOR ME GRAY
A lonesome tear trickling down a face
to join those of yesterday in salty embrace.
The trustee in gray flannel suit
playing conservatively by the rule.

COLOR ME GRAY
A venerable, acceptable non-color
smugly conforming to accepted norms.
No sun, no glow, no rainbow,
only drab, dreary, interminable gray.

I am not prepared for the emotional impact of that delivery. I feel drained. The audience reaction ranges from pity to love. The questions follow in quick succession.

"What about the Bible story of Sodom and Gomorrah? Doesn't that indicate that homosexual behavior is sinful?"

Dr. Larson comments on that question, skillfully pointing out that Lot offered the men access to his daughters. I do not remember his particular theological exegesis, but I have wrestled with those so-called proof passages from the Bible.

"The human anus is lined with a single cell fascia not designed for rough entry," opined a female doctor from the audience.

I listen to her pompous prepared remarks respectfully and then comment, "It is not my purpose to discus bedroom details of my heterosexual friends in public. I hope you will give me the same respect."

Hundreds of copies of the afternoon's proceedings are sold. I receive many e-mails and letters. Here are two:

"What meant the most to me, personally, was to hear David Larson state his own understanding of homosexuality and the Bible."

"My husband realized that he is only hurting himself by denying himself the love of his son because he is gay. He realized also how important

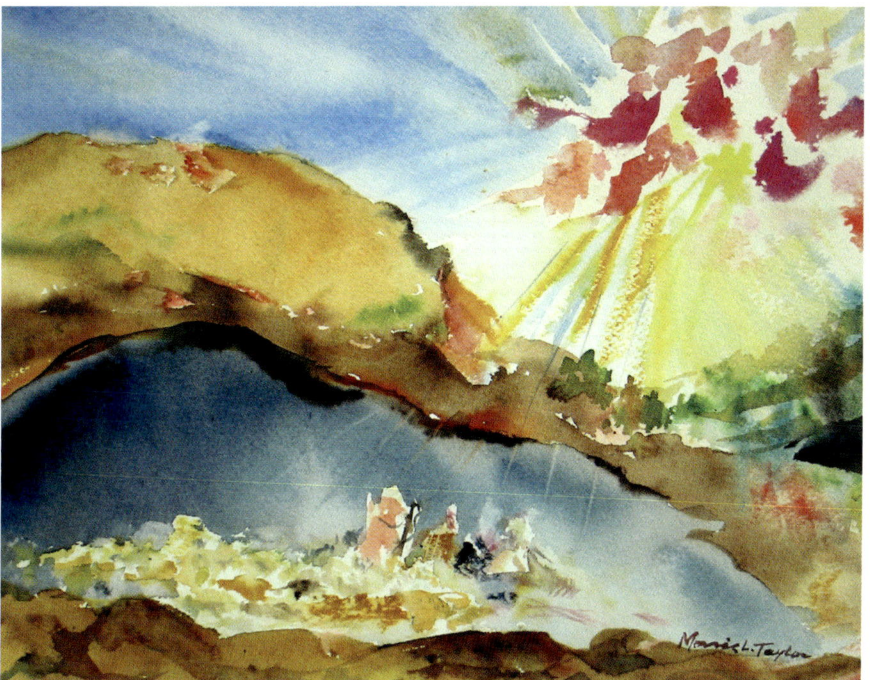

Angel's Serenade, 9 x 12

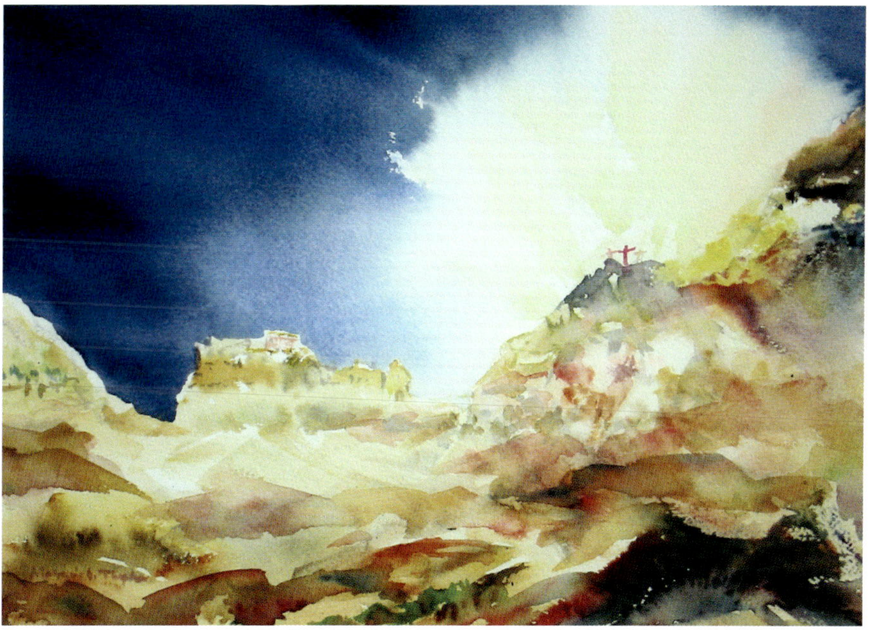

Temple Mount & Calvary, 9x12

love is and how much he wanted that love back. Today he is having lunch with Tony so he can tell him he is sorry for the hurt he has brought on them both and is asking Tony to please allow him to have the father/son relationship.”

From the congregations an older man speaks through his tears, “My lesbian daughter …” After a long pause, he tells about her struggle with the church, then continues, “She is no longer with us. Life was too intense and conflicting.”

There is nothing I can say. I resolutely step down into the audience and give this distraught father a long hug. “I know what this feels like,” I reassure him. “My gay son Leonard suicided also.”

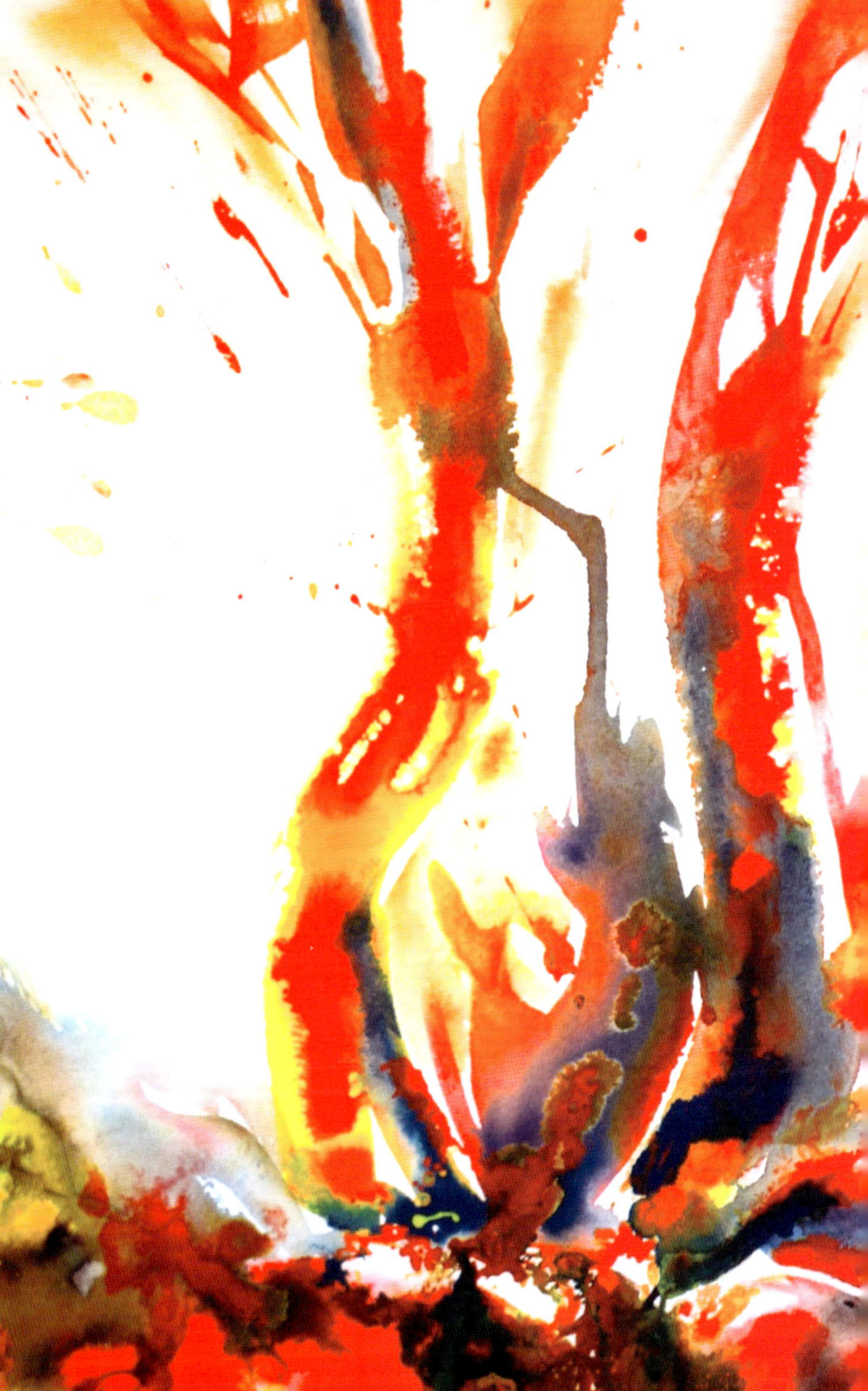

Fiery Explosion, 16 x 12

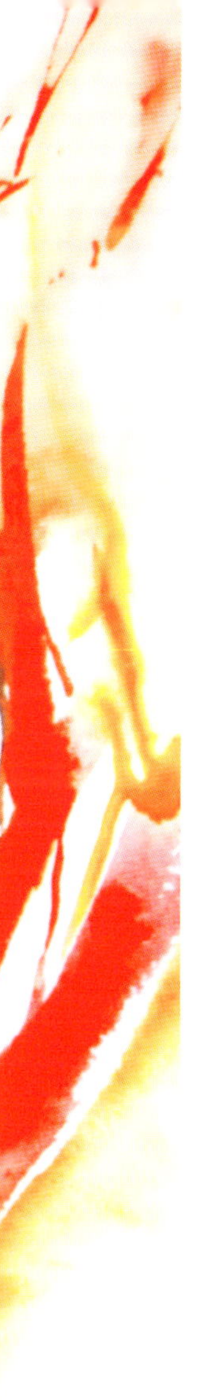

VIRGIN FIRE PLAY

Dewdrops cling to white pine trees. The five needles of each bundle hug one another to ward off the evening chill. The sap that drips freely during autumn light now congeals in darkness. In the whispering wind, my nostrils pick up the resinous scent of evergreens on the Pennsylvania hillside.

Half scared and half curious, I people-watch. Hot guys *schlepp* duffle bags, roller cases and equipment boxes down the rutted dirt road. Old-timers embrace. Even in this safe space, newcomers cower. I muse about how different these men are from the adolescents who inhabit this teen camp in summer. Playful adult males have taken over indoor gyms and outdoor pool.

"There's a first time for everything," I mutter to myself.

Taxing my social skills in the registration line, I manage, "Hi, I'm Morris." If there is a smile of recognition, I add, "Buddy, where are you from?"

One friendly person helps me find the group cabin to which I am assigned. I forget his name, but not his kindness. The Spartan dorm looks like the army barracks I had experienced at Fort Hood, Texas, many years before: the splintered and creaky floor, torn mosquito mesh on open windows, showers with unreliable hot water and little-to-no privacy.

After staking out a claim consisting of one towel hook, a clutch of coat hangers and an unpainted wooden shelf, I decide to reconnoiter. The smell of greasy food wafts from the dining room, yet no one waits in line. I wander into one of the freestanding cabins that houses a temporary commissary.

Aside from the clerk, I am alone. A few snacks are for sale, but it is the array of hemp rope, adult toys and leather gear that turns me on. I hope that my feigned nonchalance will mask my lack of experience. I enjoy fondling some of the merchandise, imagining how this flogger or that clamp will delightfully torment my body.

Sensing a dominating presence, I glance up. There stands a bearded man. My eyes take in his tight jeans, heavy boots and Master's cover—a costume favored by dominant men into leather. His black leather vest is festooned with flame-shaped appliqués in brilliant reds and yellows.

"Does your vest mean that you are into fire play?" I blurt out. My eyes fixate on the floor. I experience hot flashes. Sweat oozes from my pores.

"Yeah," the Leatherman replies in a confident voice.

"I have no experience in this kind of sadomasochistic ritual. Can I try it out?" I ask. Whatever possesses me? I am stupid as an ass and dumb as a donkey.

The command comes swiftly. "Boy, I'll expect you at midnight on the tennis court!"

Would I? Should I? Could I? I was not introduced. I don't even know his name. What if he's a pyromaniac?

I gulp down a tasteless meal in the mess hall. I pretend to organize my clothes in the bunkhouse. I cannot focus my racing thoughts. How can I crave something so dangerous? I really am playing with fire.

My mind reassures me. I have seen demos where there have been flames that have not burned or maimed the recipient. The primitive part of my brain says, You should flee from this danger. What if something went wrong that you can't control? The rational part of my mind kicks in with, You are at Gamma National camp where the players are expert and trustworthy. Yet the argument continues with the lizard-part of my brain, You ought to fight to maintain your safety.

I resolutely decide that I crave the experience of giving up control to another man whom I can trust to lead me into a unique experience of bravery, machismo and mastery of self.

Fifteen minutes to midnight I approach the abandoned tennis courts. There I undress. Darkness conceals my pile of neatly folded clothes. I put my boots back on and walk to the center of the fenced pavement of the tennis courts. Shivering and quivering, I stand naked at parade rest, legs extended with hands clenched in the small of the back. The moments stretch toward midnight.

From behind instant terror strikes: crackle of flames, searing of heat and singeing of hair. A firebrand flashes in and out of my crotch and up and down my legs. I am too scared to speak; yet, I trust this "top" who is skillfully controlling the torch.

Sensing my terror, my unseen torturer says, "Boy, you're going to be okay. I'll take good care of you."

He continues to whisk fiery wands that scorch my flesh in sensitive areas of my body. I sniff the acrid smoke and shudder. I blink when flames pierce the inky darkness. I cringe as the heat penetrates my skin. My cock rises and hormones kick in. The burns are mild. In the excitement of the scene, endorphins turn pain into pleasure. I am sexually aroused and, of course, really hot.

The mysterious man hugs me hard. I melt in his arms, exhausted and exhilarated at the same time. "Good boy. I'm proud of you," he says. "My scene name is Flash; my real name is Arthur. I already know you are Morris; your buddies said you are a serious player."

My terror has turned into trust. "Thanks, Flash. You definitely fulfilled a fantasy. Since childhood I have had a fascination with fire. I nearly set a house ablaze playing with matches. Back then I experienced nightmares of burning alive after the preachers scared me with hellfire sermons. Now it seems like my soul is purged of fear."

"Morris, I have one request," he says. "At breakfast tell me if you're still okay."

The next morning I spot Arthur's flame-decorated vest. "Flash," I say, "that was one hot scene last night. My skin is red and a bit itchy, but I feel fine. My hair will grow back. I just hope you enjoyed yourself as much as I did."

Arthur, aka Flash, reassures me, "In a couple of days, you won't see any evidence."

Proudly and defiantly I proclaim to myself, I dare to be who I am. I'm not scared of fire, not even the preacher's hellfire. I'll never be a fire play virgin again.

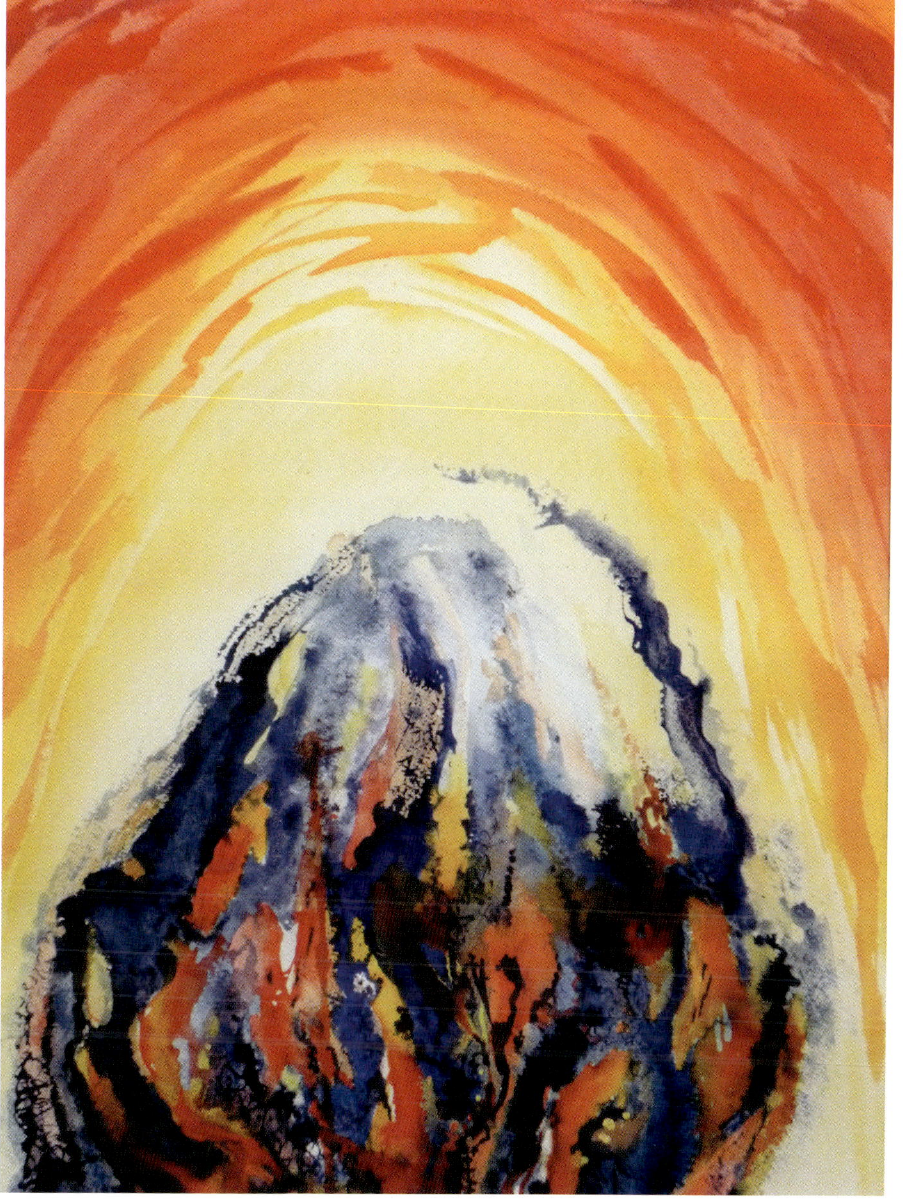

Burning Ember, 16 x 12

FIRST MASTER/SLAVE EXPERIENCE

"Strip slave!" he shouts like a true Marine major who he is. "Here are some cleaning supplies. I want this bathroom spotless. Don't forget the bowl on the floor."

Jason, my first Master, scowls as his round face and shaved head reddens. His bolt-upright posture and vigorous gestures melt my residual will. I cannot escape his blue, penetrating eyes nor ignore his manly musk.

Naked ass in the air, I scrub the floor on my hands and knees. I hear occasional taunts and feel intermittent prodding. *I didn't drive three hours for this humiliation*, I think. Yet I plunge into the dark recesses of a slave experience completely submitting myself to this Master.

I remember the brief negotiation of the week before this encounter. At that time I made two requests. Don't touch my family; I am married with four nearly adult children. Don't touch my religion; I am a professor at a church-related university. I determine to live into this scene and go through with the investigation of my inner slave and, perhaps, potential Master existence.

Back to present reality. "Thirsty?" asks Master Jason.

"Yeah. I mean, yes Sir."

"Put some water in the bowl. Lap it up!"

I'm glad that I washed that dog dish several times.

The next thing I know, I am being stuffed into an iron cage. In a cramped position I am chained uncomfortably to the bars. I am shivering. The room is chilly, but not cold.

Like an animal being punished, I am vulnerable to my tormentor. The hood makes it impossible to see, and the gag makes it impossible to speak.

Then I hear some weird music. At first I try to figure out who composed this contemporary mass. Gradually I lose organized thought, as I absorb the provocative emotions of a soul who searches for meaning. Jason, my sado-masochistic Master, had promised not to touch my religion; yet, being alone in this condition causes me to contemplate who I am, why I am here and how I can grow. I delve deep into my core spirituality and find a strange longing to escape my fundamentalist roots. I do not know how long I am shackled in this prison. My joints ache.

Upon my release from the chains, locks, hood and gag, my persecutor suspends me up on some devise in the middle of the room with my feet barely touching the floor. I can't quite remember all of the sources of pain. I am totally under my tormentor's control. What happens next is a blur.

"Clean up this mess!" The shout falls upon my already overloaded brain.

"Yes, Sir," I reply as if I were his perpetual slave.

Here I am again on my hands and knees mopping the floor. Only this time I am aroused. Now that I can speak again; I have nothing to say.

Soon I am strapped into a kind of metal chair. It is painfully upright. I can scarcely move a muscle. I am blindfolded and gagged again. A buzz. A shock wave. Now here. Now there. No part of my body is safe. A lull. I think I will faint. Surprises keep coming until I believe that I can stand no more, and yet I have to cope with the severe sensations.

"Get your clothes on, you wretched, no good slave. Go to the corner store and fetch some drinks for me."

Before I head for the stairs, he places an innocent-looking contraption on my genitals. I think this is to remind me that he owns me or maybe he just wants my cock to be at attention. Little do I know that my tormentor can shock my balls by remote control. Upon returning with the drinks, I kneel and present the libation to my master. I sense that he is pleased with me, though I dare not ask nor look at his face. I sit on the floor at my master's feet and begin to sob.

"Don't you cry on me, boy," Jason orders in a gruff voice. He puts his boot on my naked groin and presses the heel until I squirm. "You are a good slave."

Before I leave Jason gives me a big hug. This is my introduction to the Master/slave world. Not bad for the second bondage, masochistic experience ever. The minor bruises on my body heal in a couple of days. I find freedom in the reorientation of my mind. Now I dare to live into my dreams as a spiritual person who is exploring the Master/slave dynamic. I am beginning the odyssey that will lead me, two decades later, to become International Master 2013.

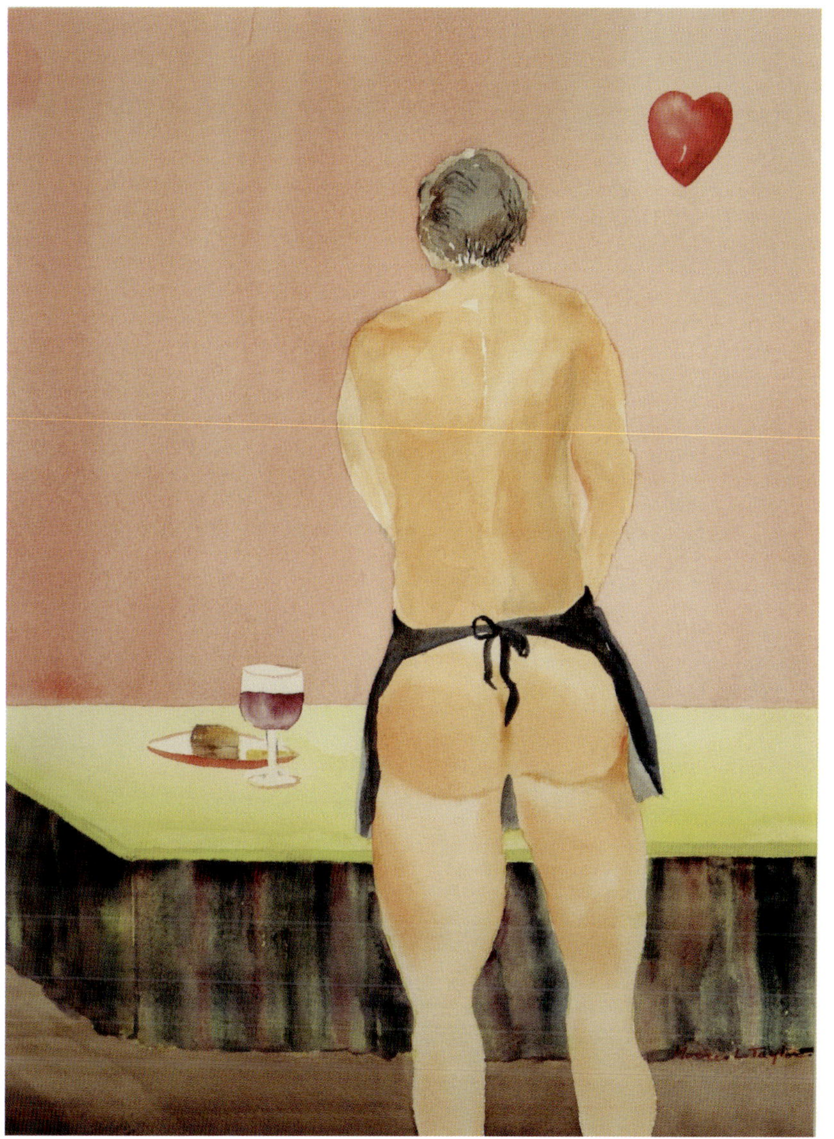

Service Is Sacred, 16 x 12

HOW DID YOU FIRST MEET?

Details are scant. I only know that the event is a men's affair and that there will likely be some sort of bondage or spanking. I wear a tight shirt, leather vest and a jacket with studs. I tuck the Levi jeans, army-style, into my boots. Will this be the day that I, a cool top, meet a hot guy?

The building on Otis Street looks rundown, a four-story industrial building that has served its purpose. At the top of a half flight of stairs, I see a raised desk. "C'mon up," the disheveled guy says. "You're in the right place."

"I hear there's a party. Have you seen a middle-aged man with a slight limp named Dick? He is supposed to meet me here at two."

"Naw," the clerk replies. "Give me the twenty dollars and go on in. I'll tell him you're here." He points down the stairwell with his crooked index finger.

"What did you say your name is?"

"He'll recognize me by Master Morris," I say. "I gave you my real name when I signed in."

The wooden stairs sag and creak as I carry my bag filled with adult toys down into the basement. A miasma of humidity and mold greets my nostrils. Gradually my eyes adjust to the semi-darkness. A few coin machines that dispense soft drinks line one wall. Turning right I see a few people lounging on old furniture. I don't recognize anyone. I settle on a bench near a post that I can lean on and loosen the top buttons of my shirt.

I don't do boring well. After about twenty minutes of waiting for Dick, I unzip my toy bag, take out a flogger and fondle it. No one takes the bait. Out of the corner of my eye I see someone amble tentatively into my space. I rise to greet him. "Hi, I'm Morris," I say. "Are you new here?"

"Yes," he replies. "I'm supposed to meet a friend, but I guess he stood me up."

"Strange; this is my first time too," I say, "and the guy that invited me has let me down. Guess we'll have to have a good time on our own. What's your name?"

"Jonathan. I need to wander off now. Maybe I'll see you later."

Feeling rejected, I wait anxiously for this handsome man to reappear. Although he is balding, I can see beneath those bushy eyebrows a noble face: prominent nose, chiseled chin and soulful eyes. His shy smile belies a strong intelligence. I determine to cross his path again, and I do.

"Neither of our friends has shown up," I say. "Would you like to play? I'm experienced and safe. What kind of things do you enjoy?"

Jonathan answers, "I like spanking. I haven't had much chance to experiment."

"Let's find a more private place to play. Follow me."

We look into a room that has no door. I remark, "That looks dingy. The furniture covers are unsanitary."

"I don't like this nook much better," says Jonathan.

Then I lose him. I know that I must pursue this potential partner.

Around the next right angle of the labyrinthine hall, I spy him again.

"I know where there is a cleaner, better lit space. You'll like it," I urge.

Jonathan follows timidly. I let him catch up to me. Then I make my move. I ask, "May I touch you?"

"Yeah, it's okay," he murmurs.

Gently I push him toward the wall. I press my body against his and rub my beard into his neck. His masculine scent is an aphrodisiac. I lift my right knee to put pressure on his quivering cock. I whisper, "You can trust me. I'll take good care of you."

"What would you like me to do?" Jonathan asks with resignation.

"Take your shirt off," I order. "The more naked you are, the more fun you'll have." Soon the submissive boy is down to his underwear. Out of the roller suitcase I take four fur-lined shackles made of leather. I fasten the straps one at a time on arms and legs. Then I gently push his body forward to a wooden St. Andrew's cross. Near the end of each bar of the X-shape are hooks, two for the upraised hands and another pair near the floor for the feet. When Jonathan's quivering body is secure, I lean in to give assurance. "You are in control of this scene. There are three words: green means, 'please more, Sir'; yellow means, 'take it easy, Sir'; and red means, 'stop now.' Do you understand?"

"Yes, Sir!" comes the quick reply.

"Don't hesitate to speak. But you do not need to say anything. I read my bottom well, and I usually know what turns you on sexually," I say.

Judging from the body feedback and the mutual response, the flogging scene is a success. We hug and talk. I start to stow the toys back in the case. I sense that something is missing. Neither of us is quite satisfied.

"What about the spanking?" Jonathan hints.

"You poor boy," I say as I reach out to pat his shapely ass. "Come over here. Lie across my knees. You deserve Master's attention." Jonathan writhes in delight and moans in painful pleasure. Exhausted we pack up the toys and head for a comfortable love seat near the bottom of the stairs. I hug Jonathan until he is relaxed. He curls up and I place my warm leather jacket over him.

"I see that you are content." I say. "My friend, Dick, has finally arrived two hours late. I see him playing in the caged area. I'll be back soon."

When I return, Jonathan snuggles close. We talk intimately about our dreams and expectations. I am looking for a permanent relationship with a submissive man of quality who will serve me well. Jonathan confesses that he has been online searching for a Master who will discipline him and lead him into a life of service. At the climax of the conversation, I dare to say, "If you were my slave you would not be sitting next to me, you would be on the floor."

Immediately, Jonathan slithers his naked body from the chair to the cold concrete floor. He kisses my right boot avidly. I gradually stand and place my left boot into the crack of his eager ass. That afternoon we progress from strangers, to play partners, to friends and progress toward becoming Master and slave. I kiss him and slap both cheeks.

As I leave Jonathan, now fully clothed, at the bus stop I command him to perform two tasks. Sensing a certain lack of self-esteem, I request he do something nice for himself every day and let me know what it is. Realizing a need for relationship building, I require that he create a secret on-line journal where he gives his new Master a daily update.

In a post the next day, June 9, 2008, my novice slave writes in a newly established, private blog, "I met a Master of Masters. We played for a single session, for a few hours, but in those few hours we had bonded and built such a trust, that—to quote Master Morris—I went from stranger to player to boy to slave in the course of that session … Master Morris made me feel not just completely at ease but free to be myself. He spoke with me very seriously about my limits, about my experience, about my needs. He executed on those so perfectly, it drove me wild with the desire to satisfy him any way I could."

Six years later, his slave's blog, along with his Master's response, has over three thousand entries, a virtual account of a great journey. The chronicle tells the truth. Jonathan and I are married and live in a twenty-four-hour, seven-day-a-week Master/slave relationship. My slave continues to write on any subject with no restrictions. Master accepts his slave as he is and replies with to the posts with candor.

The stakes are high. The overlay of the M/s life magnifies the challenges and opportunities that come with marriage. I take seriously the responsibility of mastering another human being. A person with slave instincts experiences a raw vulnerability along with an insatiable desire to serve. Before going to bed my slave kneels and confesses, "I am a loyal slave. I choose to obey my Master and to serve him to the best of my ability."

To which I improvise a reply similar to, "I accept the service of my slave and promise to protect and guide him faithfully."

During our Master/slave exchange in December of 2012, I sense that something serious is wrong. Jonathan curls up on his bed in a fetal position. He seems comatose, loath to speak. My heart leaps into my throat. I keep my composure and reassure him that everything will be all right.

By morning I feel inadequate. I realize that I do not have the resources to heal this crisis. I love the guy, and I feel guilty that I triggered this event. Jonathan has a counselor he trusts and he agrees to make an immediate appointment. I consult with another Master whom I trust. Out of respect for each other we suspend our M/s protocol. Over a period of several months each of us receives the counseling and medication we need to heal. At first we play the role of M/s at public leather events; after all are we not titleholders and leaders in the community? Gradually we phase in the protocols of our M/s life in earnest. I as Master regain my composure and energy. He as slave regains his trust and balance.

Then comes the big event when Jonathan and I compete for the title of International Master 2013 at South Plains, Texas. I quote the words of Jonathan from his daily blog "It happened. We won. I feel transformed … we did everything according to a script I did not even realize we had written. It was virtuosity without pride. It was a magnificent show without arrogance. We were ourselves. Most of all, we had fun."

FOUR HOUR ODYSSEY
a dark, dank basement
two strangers furtively circling
one grey haired, the other balding
each invited by a friend not present

eyes coyly meet
dare they speak
chit chat
this and that

the older lures the younger
a labyrinth of rooms and hopes
no place seems suitable
magnetic magic attracts

fox and rabbit
pursuit and panic
dominance and submission
desire and delight

roped to St. Andrew's cross
spanked over bony knee
enfolded in leather jacket
accepted naked on the floor

friends seek complimentary fantasies
partners ask for what they want
players dare to trust each other
brothers bond on spiritual level

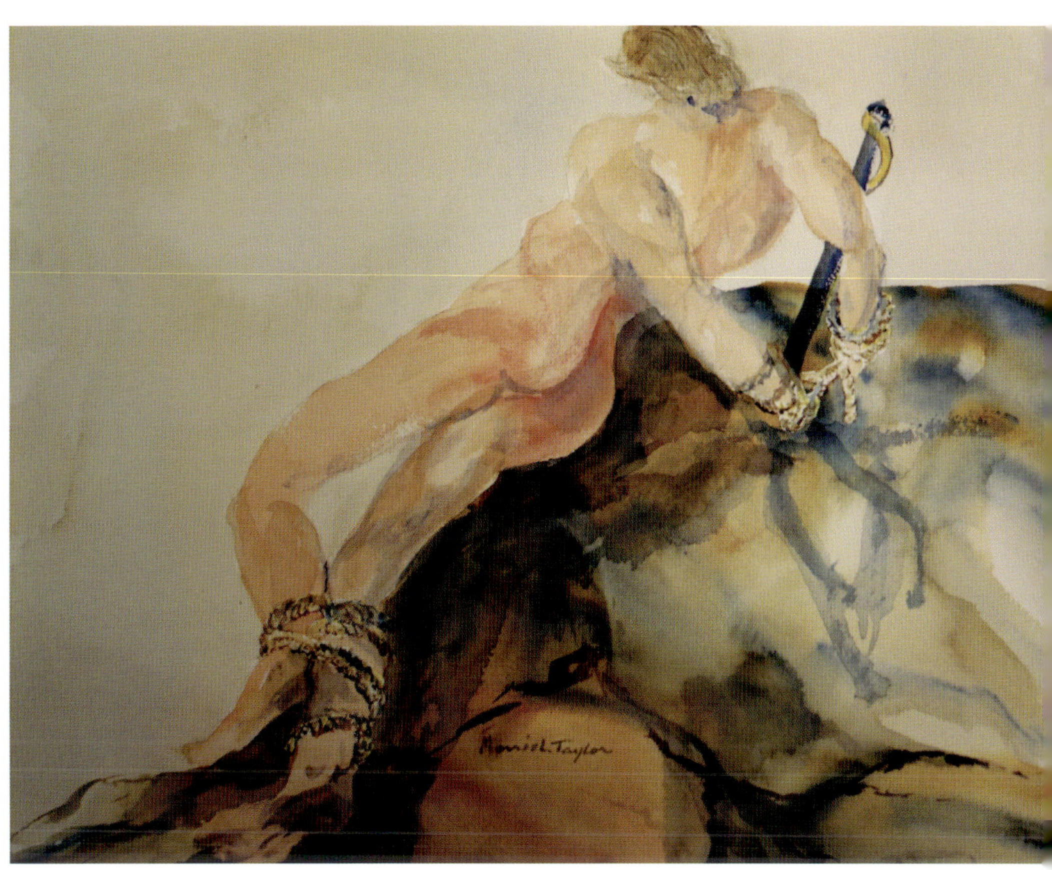

Bound Slave, 12 x 16

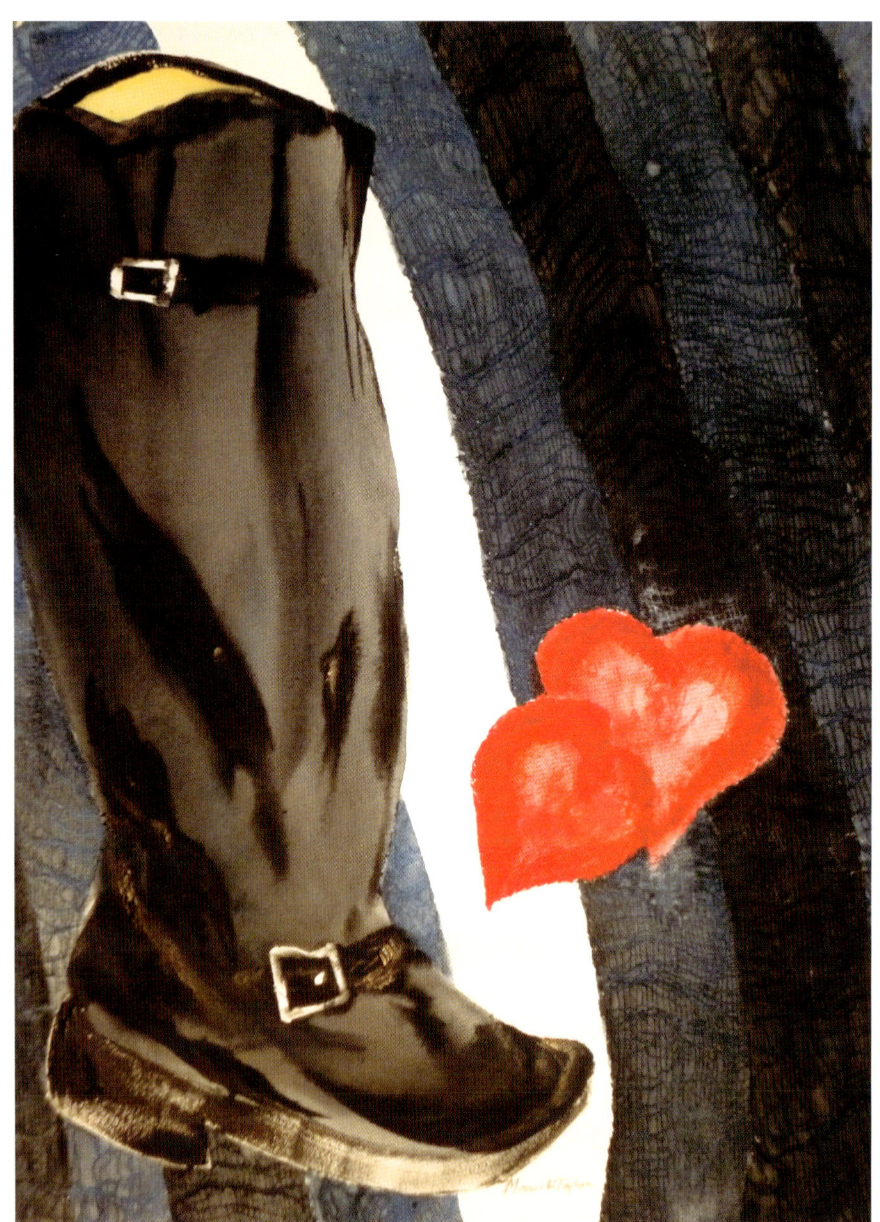

RHAPSODY TO TOM CAT

One evening cat showed up, arched his back and begged to be picked up.

Who could resist that maroon bundle with black stripes?

Presently a gentleman appeared who purported to be his keeper.

"Why don't you try him out? I know the pedigree, a rare breed."

"Tom," that was the name the guy used, "belongs to a special litter of six."

Well, I have to admit, it was love at first sight.

After fondling Tom for quite a while, I concluded that he should stay put.

Besides, my life was already complex, and I didn't have room for one more.

Glancing over my shoulder, there was Tom begging to come along.

Maybe I should return to fetch this cat and give him a home.

Leather Flag, 30 x 22

A fortnight later, you guessed it, in the same location, Tom appeared.

His back arched as before, but this time he rubbed against my leg.

My heart melted, and I fondled him like an old friend.

The owner was nowhere in sight, I picked him up and petted him gently.

How that cat writhed in my hands endearing himself to his prospective Master!

"Okay, Tom Cat, come home with me. I promise to take good care of you.

Before I do, you need to prove yourself, my little kitty.

Let's see how well you can scratch my slave's back."

As I warmed up the elegant creature, cat performed effortlessly.

Love at first handling. "Why live without you, whip with nine tails?"

"My slave just loves you, dearest Tom Cat, and I do too.

You curl around and caress a man's back with effortless strokes."

Cat enjoys scratching with uncut claws until red welts appear.

This creature has the hauteur of an Abyssinian purebred.

But behold the pleasurable pain and hark to the purrs of my beloved slave!

SILENCE

    Ssh. Quietly wait
    No need to speak
    Silence your thoughts
        Master will envelope his slave

OBEDIENCE

    Aah! Calmly acquiesce
    No decision is necessary
    Fulfill your potential with dignity
        Master will empower his slave

TRUST

    Ooh! Gently relax
    No fear or resistance
    Accept pain with pleasure
        Master will inspire his slave

SERVICE

    Umm! Eagerly serve
    No sensual treat withhold
    Sublimate your own desires
        Master will enthrall his slave

COMPLETE

    Yeah! Happily accept
    No reservation of spirit
    Occupy the deep, resonant void
        Master will encompass his slave

CANCER

The February sun is setting on Friday the thirteenth, 2015. While I play the piano, Jonathan prepares a Sabbath meal of my favorite foods in our remodeled kitchen. The phone rings.

"Hello. Morris speaking."

"This is Dr. Leung. I'm afraid that I have bad news," he says. "The Cat scan reveals cancer cells in your bone marrow and an egg-size stone in your bladder. I'm making appointments for you with an oncologist and a urologist."

I am stunned.

The windows in the living room rattle. Gusts of wind blow sheets of rain against the panes. Body discomfort gives me the only warning that this malady is upon me. I don't like the fact that malignant cells in my bones are gnawing away at my life-giving red and white blood cells.

My son, Lyndon, calls moments later to inquire about my health. "Hi, dad," he says. "Any news about your medical tests?"

"Yes, my primary care doctor called a few minutes ago. Bad news. The diagnosis is multiple myeloma. I don't know much about this disease. I have no idea about treatment or longevity."

"Let me know, dad, how I can help. I can come right away if you need me. Hopefully, it is not the fast growing kind."

Putting on a courageous front I say, "Don't worry. I'll *make the best of the situation.* No one can tell if I have six week or six months to live."

Jonathan comforts me. "You're taking this better than I am. We're in this together for the long haul. Maybe it will be six years."

I sit in my newly acquired reclining chair. The soft leather cushions feel good on my back. The burnt orange color pleases me.

Jonathan asks, "Which Mahler symphony?"

I choose the second, subtitled, "Resurrection." Simon Rattle conducts the Berlin Philharmonic streaming into our room via Internet.

The first movement acknowledges the ominous pain. So direct are the simple pleasures of life in the second movement. In the third I hear the wry moments, the quirky good times. The inexorable climax of life grabs hold of me as the music alternates between despair and hope. In the last movement of this gigantic symphony Mahler celebrates life, death and resurrection.

This magnifying lens of life-threatening illness focuses my attention upon a life well spent. Now the few years ahead beckon me to be brave and to live honorably. I deserve a Sabbath rest.

I intend to continue to emphasize the beautiful things in my life as long as I have energy. On Wednesday, I will deliver two commissioned watercolors. I am negotiating with the Leather Archives & Museum in Chicago regarding a one-person show. Jonathan promises to complete or use the material of my memoir now in progress, *Nine Lives of Morris.* Before going to bed an e-mail invites me to play some piano music for a banquet in a few weeks. My garden will get along with less attention; I don't kneel well, but I can reach the flowerpots.

Over the years I have been kind to persons in need. A dozen or so relatives, students and friends have been welcomed into our home for periods of time. My parenting and teaching have their own rewards. Now I must accept more frequently the kindness of others. With grace I plan to take only what I need. Instead of "why me," "why not me?" I am having a good life far above what I expect or deserve.

The weekend is long, full of foreboding. The search for the best doctor to treat my cancer begins in earnest. I decide to wait three weeks for an appointment with the head of the Kaiser department. Dr. Lint says that he needs a bone biopsy in addition to an MRI to definitively diagnose my condition. I am eager to know the result of this painful test and to begin treatment. To my dismay my oncologist leaves for a four-week vacation without discussing the results of the tests or outlining the treatment plan to me.

Jonathan and Larry urge me to attend the International Myeloma Society meetings. I demand copies of my Kaiser medical records. While the general and plenary sessions are helpful, the private meeting with Dr. Drurie, president of the worldwide organization, proves to be reassuring. In twenty minutes he peruses the folio of documents, all the while relating pleasantly to me.

"You are fortunate," says the doctor. "Your myeloma in Stage One. With proper treatment you should look forward to many years ahead."

"Thank you sir," I reply. "No one has given me that hope. I thought maybe my life expectancy was six weeks or six months."

Dr. Drurie adds, "The analysis of your biopsy reveals that your particular type of cancer is one of the less aggressive ones. You are in Stage One, which is treatable, not curable. I believe you will continue to play the piano, paint watercolors and anything else you are healthy enough to enjoy."

Good news. Even when I suffer backaches and my body is weary, I find new hope. The treatments and side effects are often unwelcome events. The most expensive and effective drug, Revlimid, causes major allergic reactions. Now I take a trio of medications by mouth and by infusion that keep the bad cells from taking over my bone marrow. Radiation of some vertebra eases the back pain. Despite chronic fatigue I am active doing the things I enjoy most. Life goes on, maybe to a hundred years old.

Hummingbird and I Fly Away
I planted that red-orange milkweed,
nectar for your flight.
Dare on tip of agave spear
whirring wings to rest?
You and I are tired
of constant search for energy
to keep in motion
until we find another garden.
Neighbors say,
"We'll miss you when you're gone."
Is this the day
when the spectral sun
turns our aging, dark feathers
into an iridescent, transcendent, exit into eternity?

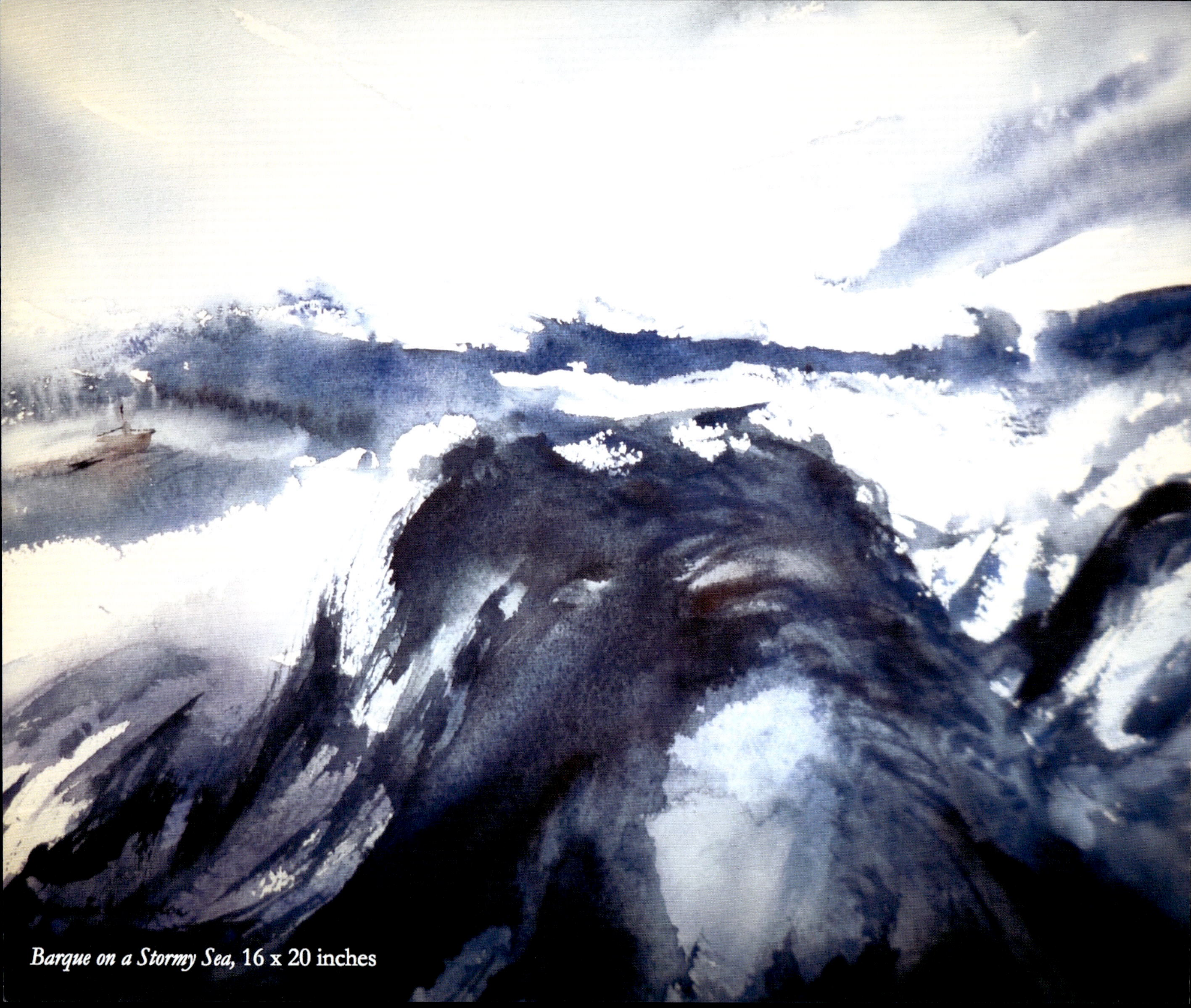

Barque on a Stormy Sea, 16 x 20 inches

WATER OF LIFE

I

Embryo
beginning of life
floating toward birth

jolted into breathing
air filtered
by watery lungs

cries for mother's
nipple
teary cheek

wet diaper
drooling mouth
demand attention.

II

Thirsty child
fresh from sport
quaffs liquid

to grown sinew
to sweat
salty toxins

to control tantrums
reach exhaustion.
My, how you've

grown tall,
learned to swim and
bathe yourself!

III

Productive adult
builds aqueducts
to irrigate crops

and natatoriums
to train for Olympics
float or sink

compete or fail
rip tide
deluge unexpected

today global
climate erratic
rainbow tomorrow.

IV

Be baptized
evangel of doom.
Watery grave

or new life?
Mature judgment
surfs above

storm surge.
I am not stoned:
drink to

atoning grace.
Engulf me,
Water of Life.

Written by Morris L. Taylor on Friday, the thirteenth, 2015, upon learning of a cancer diagnosis.

Nine Lives at the Wedding

"What do you think of this place?" I ask my fiancée, Jonathan, as we walk into the large hall.

Jonathan replies. "There are no stairs; one can enter right off the street."

I take in the stained glass windows, the beamed ceilings. "I like the open space with wooden beams and hardwood floor," I say.

"I like the privacy of the balcony area," Jonathan adds. "It will be great for the collaring ceremony."

"I'm surprised. How come you're so touchy about that?" I ask.

"Master, I don't want my professional friends to see a leather collaring ceremony," my slave gently pushes back.

"I know that you are sensitive about receiving a collar in front of your colleagues," I respond. "I feel that way about my grown children and grandkids, not to mention the church people. They just wouldn't understand why we think that a chain around your neck with a lock means more to us than a wedding ring, but for once in my life I would like to create a space where all aspects of my life can be transparent. Can't we plan a reception where all feel comfortable and welcome?"

"Let's talk about that later," says Jonathan. "Right now we need to decide if The Chapel works for the wedding reception."

I reach for Jonathan's hand. He pulls away. "You're right," I agree. "Let's focus on evaluating the space."

Purposely changing the subject, I continue, "You know us Taylors; we have to celebrate with music. My three living children will be here and will play their stringed instruments. If we can only find someone to play the spot vacated by Leonard's absence; I would be so thrilled. Then I could play the Schumann's *Piano Quintet* with my children."

"When was the last time you did that?" asks Jonathan.

"The kids and I haven't played together as a family for at least twenty years."

Jonathan glances out of the corner of his eye and says, "I think this is the gal in charge striding from the bar."

"Judging from her focused stride and officious demeanor," I say, "She's the one in charge. Check out that zebra-striped dress and yesterday's platform shoes."

"Shh, being catty again, Sir," says Jonathan.

In his excitement Jonathan walks ahead to greet her. "Ahem" is all I need to do to remind him of our protocol. He must always walk a half step behind his Master. This is the covert public display of our relationship.

As the manager make an approach, she holds out her hand and says, "Hi, I'm Ms. Primrose. I assume that you are the guys that are getting married."

"Yes, ma'am," I say. "Meet my fiancée, Jonathan. I hope that …"

"That's not a problem in San Francisco," says the manager without missing a beat.

We walk toward the foot of a stage area and find an

upright piano. I ask the manager, "Is this a piano we can use and can we hoist it up to the stage?"

"Yes, and we will have it tuned as part of the rental fee," she says.

"I'm planning for an art show also," I add. "Where would we exhibit the watercolors? Along these shelves on either side of the auditorium?"

"And chairs?" Jonathan asks. "Many of the older guests will want to sit for the short programs."

"Yes, on both counts. You can use the shelves, and we have thirty-five chairs," the manager replies. "We'll bring our the high stools and the bar tables, also."

"Sir, I think that will be just right," Jonathan says to me. "Not all the two hundred guests will be here at the same time. After the reception we can dismiss the 'vanilla' guests and invite our leather friends to the collaring ceremony upstairs in the lounge area of the balcony," he adds in a soft aside. "Let's ask about the food catering. We can work out the details of combining both the wedding blessing and the collaring ceremony later."

"Is this a good time to talk about the food for the reception?" I ask Ms. Primrose.

"Yes," she says. "But let me tell the master chef that you are here. He's busy, but I'm sure he will take time to discus the options and prices. It will take about ten minutes or so."

"Somehow, I just don't feel right about dividing our friends into categories," I murmur when she leaves. "All my life I have had to be careful about separating who knows what about me. This once, I would love to have everybody be on the same page. At age eighty-two what do I have to hide? But I don't want to stress your professional life with revelations about our private lifestyle." I add, understanding my intended's reticence.

"Sir," Jonathan responds respectfully, "I want to please you, but I'm squeamish about how my professional colleagues will react when they discover I'm into leather.

"The guests need not know the details of what we do," I say quietly. "For some the wearing of leather is only fashion or fetish. For others, even those who don't wear leather, this lifestyle centers around rowdy and boisterous sex. Mixed in are varying degrees of consensual sado-masochistic behavior. Like I say, it's not that big a deal to most people."

"Yeah," responds Jonathan. "My Master always seems to be a step ahead of me."

"My dear slave, your Master wants this reception to be a happy time for everyone, especially you. I know you will do what I ask, but I will never ask you to something that I haven't done or wouldn't do. It is your duty to keep me informed about your needs and desires."

"Thank you, sir." Jonathan responds with bright eyes and a sigh. "I am fortunate to have a reliable Master who takes such good care of me."

"No, it is I who am blessed beyond measure to have a loyal slave who chooses to obey his Master," I respond.

Jonathan's body relaxes as I give his hand a squeeze. I let go as I see the chef and manager approaching.

The manager has a ready answer for our concerns about a broadly acceptable menu. "Our kitchen can arrange a vegetarian spread, a choice of food that will please everyone. We will provide an array of exotic fruits, seasonal vegetables, gourmet cheeses with hummus and mixed nuts within the budget you suggest.”

“That’s excellent. What about drinks?” I ask. “I want everyone’s glass to look the same. Champagne flutes for all: sparkling water, sparkling juice or sparkling wine?”

“I think we can arrange that,” the manager replies as she points to the adjacent room. “If they want other drinks, there is a full bar available there—their nickel.”

“Thanks a lot, ma’am,” I conclude. “I think The Chapel and the services you offer coincide with our ideas about a good time for all.”

We book the venue and start planning the guest list.

As the reception day approaches, the Southern California continent is the first to arrive. My son, Lyndon, shows up with his wife, Beth, and their two children, Rilla and Elissa and his violin. Lucy, my daughter comes with her viola. Lowell and his wife Melissa arrive by air from Pittsburgh, Pennsylvania; we rent a cello for Lowell to play. Then their childhood friend, Dawn Harms, who plays the violin professionally in the Bay Area, joins us. The evening before the big night, we practice the Schumann *Piano Quintet* at the house that Jonathan and I share on Pond Street in San Francisco’s Castro. We sound a little rusty, but the players loosen up and hit their stride.

Intent as I am on the practice I look around to see how Jonathan reacts to this intense concentration. First I notice that he is filming the rehearsal with his iPhone. Then he is sitting on the floor by me, a gesture that speaks of his devotion. This is a low protocol way of proclaiming to our family the joy we experience together as Dominant and submissive.

“Dad, how come you didn’t sound this good when we were kids,” my daughter asks with undiplomatic generosity. Her brothers are shocked.

I can’t let this go without a comeback, “Lucy, when you were kids, I made the lunches and earned the living while you practiced,” I explain. “Now, at last I have time.”

When the celebration day dawns, I have hardly slept. I do my usual half hour of exercises and take a bath in my jet tub before anyone else is awake. Though I present a calm exterior, my heart races with excitement. A lifetime dream is about to be realized. People from all aspects of my life are coming to our party. Taking a deep breath I tell myself, *Your job is to make everyone feel welcome. Just enjoy. You deserve it.*

I prepare a favorite family breakfast of waffles with mashed bananas and chopped walnuts in the batter. Bowls of fruit decorate the kitchen table. The family wearily gathers and starts eating. Then the doorbell rings. Friends show up for a morning bite. They join us at the overcrowded kitchen table. We eat in shifts.

“Glad to see you all,” I say as my slaves bring more waffles and make more coffee. “These are some of my leather friends,” I add, kind of apologizing for their vests, 501 jeans, boots and tattoos.

One friend has a solid brass collar around his neck and an obvious nose ring. When I introduce him to my daughter-in-law, Beth, she says enthusiastically, “They’re part of our family.” Everyone has a good laugh and digs into the food.

Lucy, always a vocal host says, “We know about dad’s leather friends. We’re proud of him.”

"Lyndon, are you ready to pick up the flowers?" I ask my youngest son.

"Yes, Dad. I parked our car so I can get out early," he responds.

"The dealer at the farmer's market promised a good supply at seven this morning," says Beth.

"The vases and floral putty are on the table in the garden. Remember when I did the flowers for your wedding?" I say.

My daughter, Lucy, is already being hostess. "Dad, it's Lowell and Melissa arriving."

"Tell them to come to the table, Lucy. The next batch of waffles is ready to serve. Do you remember that you are in charge of the music, the stands and setting up the stage? We can't get into the venue until noon. The guests might arrive early."

"Stop worrying, Dad," she replies. "I've got everything under control."

My son, Lowell, comments as he slathers his waffle with butter and maple syrup, "I have the list. Take it easy and enjoy. This is your day."

The doorbell rings again. It's Jonathan's friend Don, who shows up with his truck. We load a huge orchid plant from my backyard garden, a big cymbidium with dozens of blooms, and other plants for the stage.

"Don't forget the cement urn and the New Zealand pine from the garden," I tell Don. "They go on the stage. Don't hide the musicians. Check to be sure there is a live mic available."

Larry, who lives in his own condo in the city, arrives and enters without knocking. After introducing him all around as part of my family, I issue special orders. "Your job is be the point-man seeing that everything is coordinated and everyone is welcome."

With his usual efficiency he whispers in my ear, "Did you hear that the flower seller never appeared with your order? Lyndon and his wife have been going all over the town to find some florists open this early on Sunday morning."

Almost on cue, Lyndon and Beth calmly appear with armloads of flowers: my favorite gladiolas, golden-hued roses and lots of greenery.

"May I write you a check?" I ask.

"No," comes the response. "The flowers are a gift."

Over the weekend I have the opportunity to introduce my living children to many people. While I am so proud of my children's professional achievements, I am more thrilled that they are real people with distinct personalities. I appreciate how they have come from different perspectives to accept my evolution. Here they are at my same sex wedding.

Lucille Ann, my oldest child, oozes with talent and personality. As a violist, she is a soloist, chamber player, conductor and teacher. Lucy organizes the international viola congress at the Redlands University and tours sometimes with the Los Angeles Philharmonic and other orchestras. She is fluent in Spanish and was on the faculty of the Universidad of Montemorelos in Mexico.

My son, Lowell, occupies the Heinz Chair at Carnegie Mellon. For a time he was on President Clinton's board of economic advisors. His wife, Melissa, leads the nursing research team for the Veteran's Administration for a several state area. Their two children, Evan and Sarah, are high achievers. Following in their father's footsteps, they earn doctorates in economics under full scholarship from the University of Michigan.

Lyndon flips from a scholarship path for a double doctorate in medicine and pharmacology at Loma Linda University to pursue his first love, a violin performance doctorate from Juilliard. He is principal second violinist of the Los Angeles Philharmonic and formerly one of the principal concertmasters of the New Zealand Orchestra. Elizabeth, his wife, teaches at La Sierra University and publishes books on spirituality in the nursing profession. Their older daughter is a high school scholar in Stanford's online program. Elissa combines completing her preparatory education while preparing for a scholarship program in ice hockey on the college level.

Jonathan and I slip into our dressy-casual outfits— sport coats with no ties. Jonathan hates neckties. When we arrive at The Chapel on Valencia Street, our crew has already entered. Friends from the leather community help with set up. Dylan, a trans man, a special friend of our family, is on a high ladder hanging an antique Kashmiri tapestry for the stage.

"I want it really high and centered," I explain. "That's just right. You know it is a Jewish tradition to have a *chuppah*. Although this is not quite a canopy, this tradition is important to Jonathan, and I take pleasure in honoring his heritage."

Other friends from the leather community take their assigned places. Rich from Chicago, along with Jack and Lyle from the East Bay, are in charge of the selection of my watercolors. Alexandria and her leather Daddy give orders on where to place the flowers, how to hang the coats and when to serve the food.

Already a motley group of friends are lined up at the door: gay men in leather jackets and boots, church folks dressed to the nines, professional colleagues in business casuals with neckties and a transgendered Rabbi dressed in full leather and a bikers cap. I decide to let them in early even though we aren't quite ready. Most of them make a beeline to the gift table to select one of the free floral watercolors I have painted. Rich comes over to me and says, "Morris, there is some polite fighting going on."

I think all one hundred and fifty of them, which have taken me two years to paint, will be taken home this afternoon. Several people buy framed watercolors and giclée copies of my masterpieces, *Creative Energy and Destructive Power*. I am delighted that my friends desire a piece of my artistic energy. I get a high from giving and seeing people accept that part of myself. "I love to make people happy," I say. "I only wish that I could see which painting each guest chooses."

In the same room with the paintings I spy the dessert table. "Hey, look at this, you guys," I shout. "Just what we ordered, apple tart tatin and black forest cherry torte. Aren't they luscious looking?"

In walks a tall Dutchman with two small children. Jonathan's ex-husband has travelled here from Amsterdam, The Netherlands, where he lives with their daughters, Sarah, age nine and Esther, age six. The girls are exuberant. Jonathan's ex-partner, Minne, is at first uncomfortable. As colleagues and friends whom he recognizes congregate, he loosens up. I notice him smiling as he talks with them and sips champagne.

I get so busy welcoming guests that I loose track of time. My daughter, Lucy, warns me, "Dad, you need to get ready to play the Schumann. You're having too much fun talking to your friends." *That's a twist. All these years of concerts, and now my child tells me when to go on stage,* I think.

I quickly get to the piano. A chill ripples down my spine as I join my three children: Lyndon, violin; Lucy, viola; and Lowell, cello, joined by Dawn, violin. My page-turner is Art, one of my star piano students from Andrews University in Berrien Springs, Michigan.

A crowd gathers in the beamed auditorium. Some stand; others are seated. This is the first time that the Taylor String Quartet and I have performed since my son Leonard committed suicide in his mid-thirties. I am overcome with emotion, which I pour into the performance. The adrenalin kicks in as we reach the finale. The audience, which make up of the most diverse group of people I have seen anywhere, applauds as one.

During the interval between the music, Jonathan introduces me to his professional guests. "Meet Jane Bronstein, she is a founding member of Chi, the international design group that I attended in Paris and Beijing. And this Raphael, my former boss at Google."

"Pleased to meet you," I say. "Jonathan speaks highly of you. Thanks for being part of our celebration."

Now it's my turn. "Jonathan, I would like you to meet some of my friends from Grace Cathedral. This man is an Adventist pastor. Here is one of my former students from Andrews University. The lady in the mobile chair with her dog attended an Adventist academy and married the organist whom we heard play at the Legion of Honor. Later they divorced, and the lady seated next to her is now her lesbian wife. I'll save that story for later."

"You better get the music started," says Jonathan.

"Don't worry." I respond. "Lowell is acting as emcee. I see him going to the stage now. Let's sit down and soak in the rest of the musical tributes."

For the second act each of the young musicians serenades the bridal couple with solos. Jonathan and I beam from the first row center. Lowell comes to the microphone to propose a toast. Everyone raises a glass in honor of our marriage.

The best moment is saved for last. Jonathan has consented to holding our collaring marriage ceremony in the presence of all. We have come up with some novel adaptations of the solemn leather ceremony. This will be a first for many in the room.

The rainbow of our beliefs is represented. Rev. Fox from the Night Ministry, which provides crisis intervention and social services in San Francisco, blesses our marriage in the Episcopal manner. Rabbi Joel, a longtime friend from the leather community in Philadelphia explains the origin of the Wedding Kaddish and intones the prayer as adapted for a gay union.

Then comes the big moment. To Jonathan and me, and to our friends from the leather community, a collaring means more than the exchange of rings. Jonathan accepts me as his Master acknowledging that he submits to my leadership, discipline and ownership. I take charge of his life, devoting my best energies for the benefit of our relationship and well-being. My Master instincts demand that my slave and I will be greater than the sum of us both and more fulfilled as we live into our true selves as Dominant and submissive.

Jonathan's two adopted daughters, Sarah and Esther, are our sweet collar bearers. They hand each of us the tokens of our love. One holds a gold necklace, the other a silver necklace with a padlock. Jonathan and I face each other on the stage.

Jonathan kneels, and members of the leather community gasp. They also were expecting a private ceremony. Our other guests take the ceremony in stride. Gently, I place a silver chain about Jonathan's neck and click the sterling lock in place. I reach around to embrace him and say, "I bestow this collar as a symbol of your permanent service to me. I promise to protect and guide you as long as I live. I love you as my own soul." I stand while jonathan, now permanently my slave deserving a small "j", places a gold chain about my neck accepting me as his Master. "You are holy to me," he says. The leather community is astounded that we dare to perform this collaring ceremony in public. The rest of the guests are touched by what seems like an intimate vow of extraordinary affection and commitment.

Jonathan and I stamp on the wine glass, a Jewish tradition symbolizing our new union. Glass shatters. Cheers rise. Champagne corks pop. Celebration permeates the air. *Can this be real?* I wonder. *Is this happening to me?* I am so happy. Hugs are everywhere—a rainbow of colorful characters from each of my nine lives. Everyone seems to be hugging someone near him or her out of pure joy.

A line quickly forms. My sixth sense knows that most of the people waiting to greet me have been soaking in music, art and love all afternoon. Hairy guys tickle my neck with their beards. I relish leather and sweat close to my nostrils. Salty tears of joy trickle down my face joining those of persons important to my life in the Adventist church. As a gay man I am being smothered with full bosom hugs and enjoying them. Some cute young guys that I have played with at leather parties hug me real close in appreciation for my mentorship. I love huge bear hugs. Clergy persons from many traditions embrace me body and soul, allowing me to accept myself and face my destiny. When my children, their wives and their children give me hugs of familial love, I remember my determination to break the cycle of hug deprivation in my family. The four slaves, all present and whose service I treasure, are giving me permitted hugs that penetrate my Master's heart. There is no greater bliss. I have just married the man of my life to hug and to hold for all the days stretching into the rainbow hued future. I embrace my nine lives as one: Yankee musician spiritual father professor artist writer gay Master.

Napa Valley Winery, 22 x 30 ►

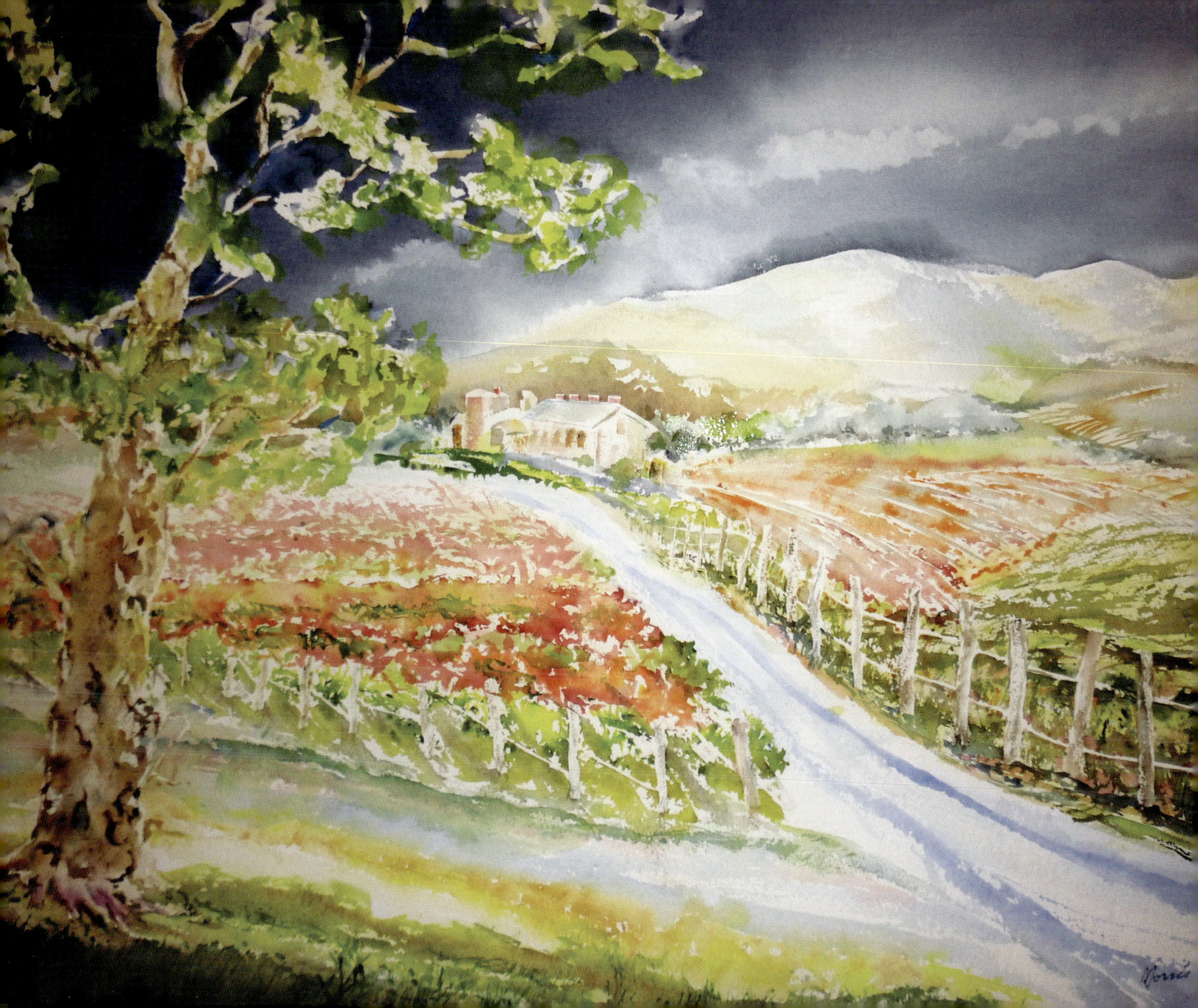

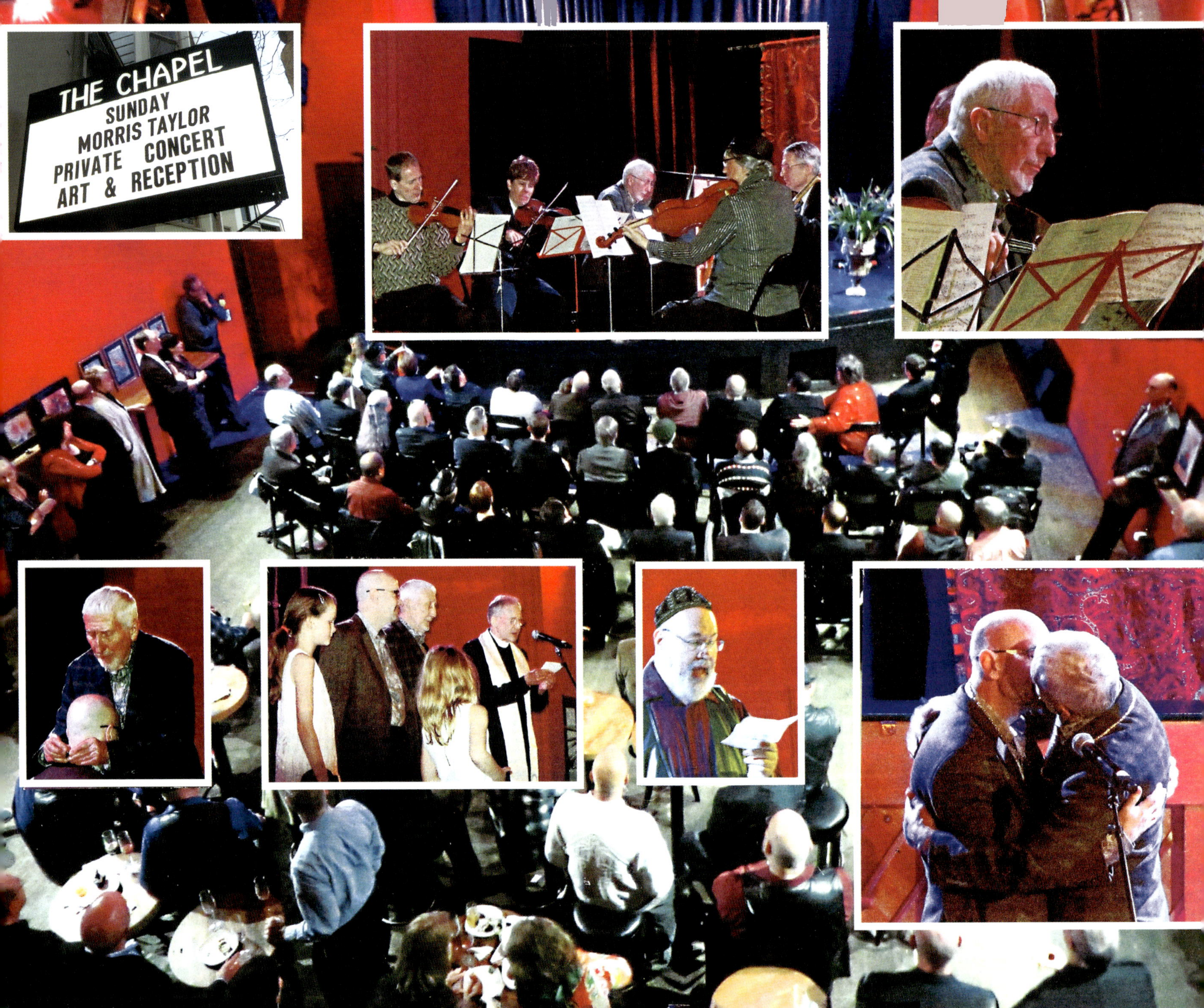
THE CHAPEL
SUNDAY
MORRIS TAYLOR
PRIVATE   CONCERT
ART & RECEPTION

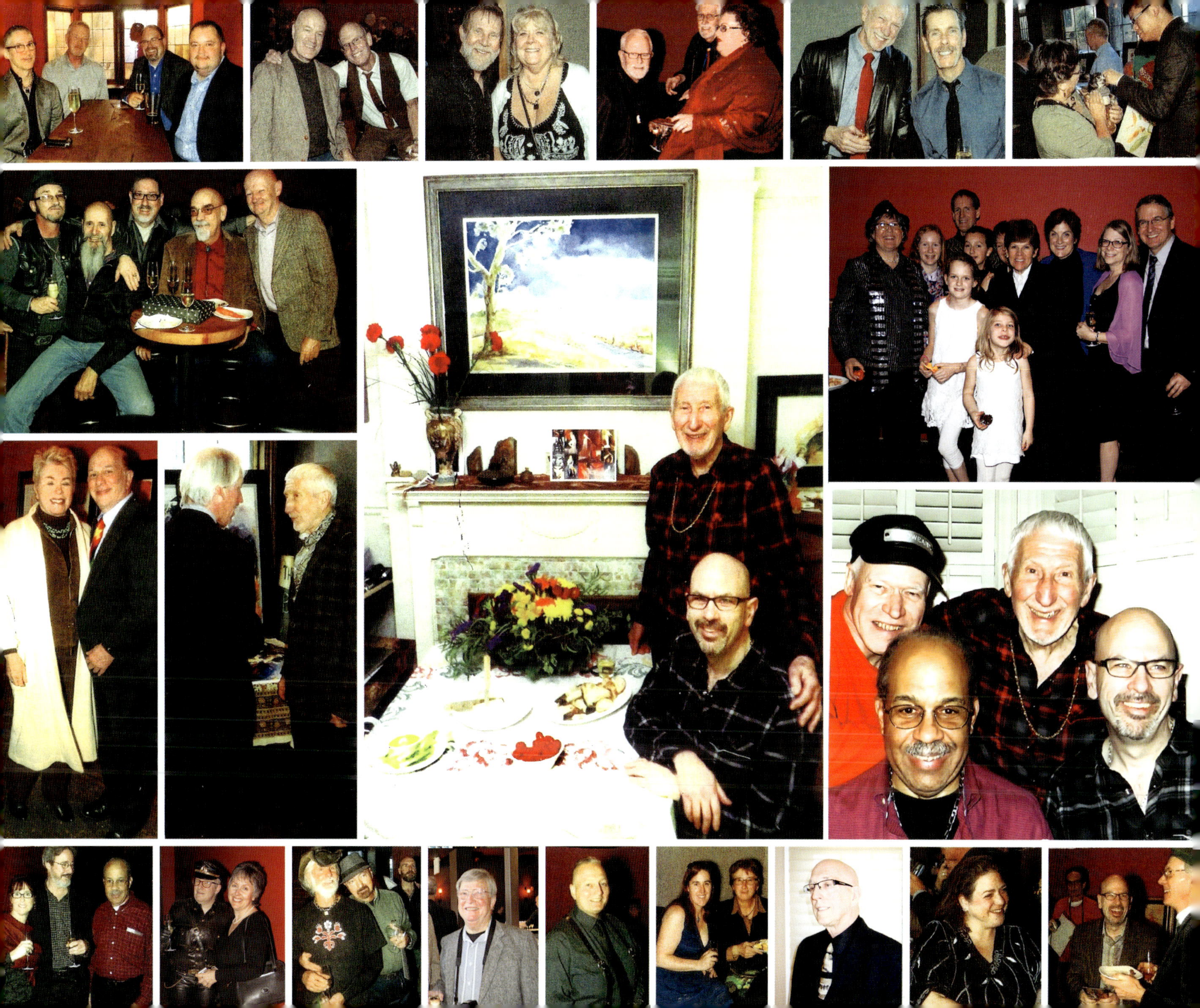

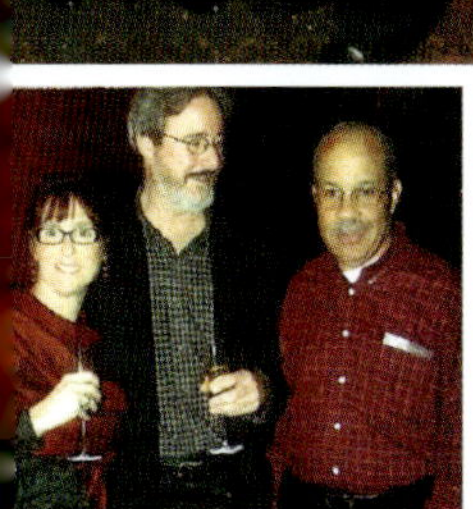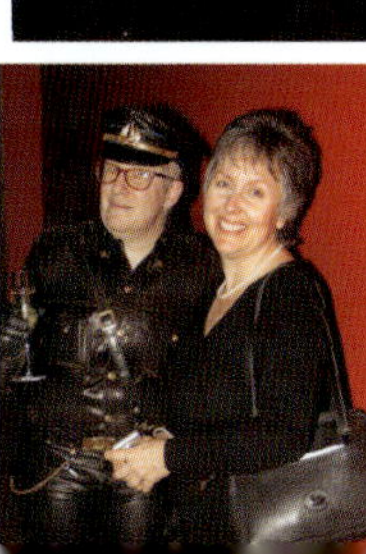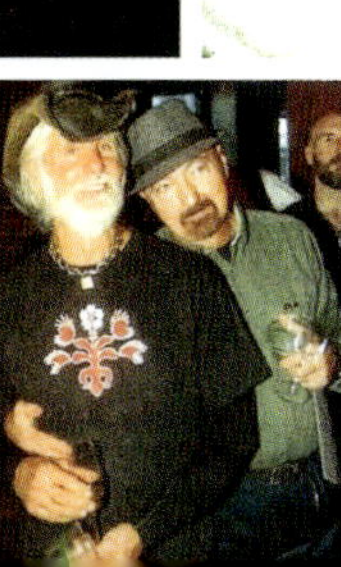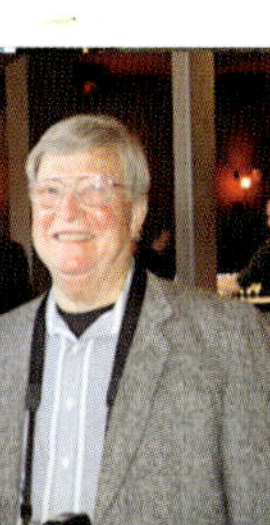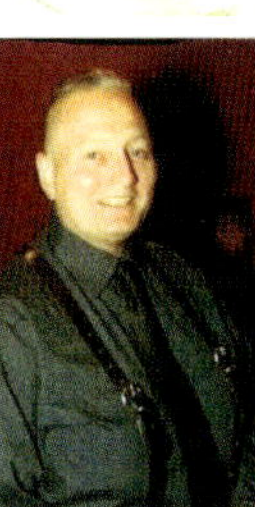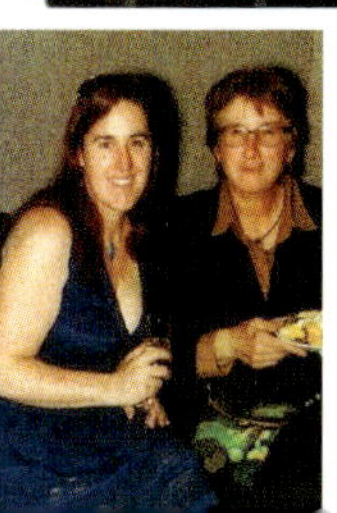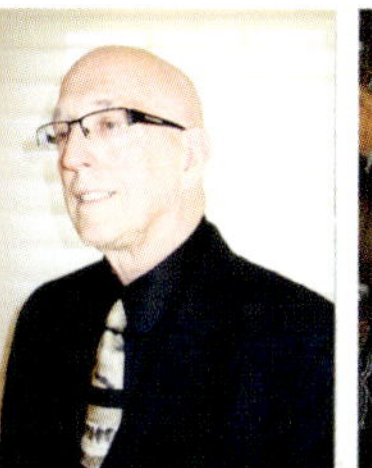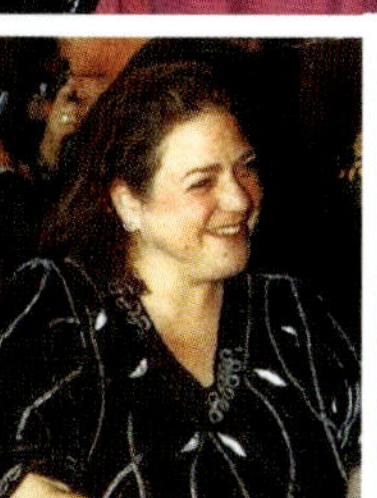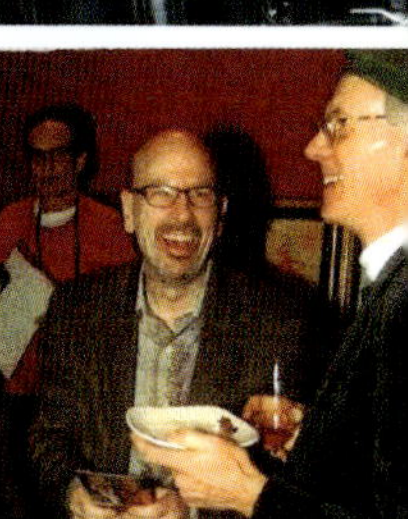

ACKNOWLEDGEMENTS

Henry and Justin Sabia-Tanis
Jonathan Arnowitz Taylor
Lawrence Brown
David M. Ortmann, LCSW
Sir Gareth and toi
Richard Bushroe and Richard Anderson
Stefano Olla
Lyndon Johnston Taylor
Anonymous
Charles E. Dee "Chuck"
William Devlin
Jonathan Domash
Thomas Peterson
Eric and Tracy Wolf
Denise Pinhey
H. M. Prestage
George Royer
Lucy Taylor
Lowell and Melissa Taylor

Evert-Ben van Veen
Michael and George
Shelly Maxie
Sage Brown and Laine Mejin
Dawn Harms
Rich Brooks
John Pointer and Gary Jennings
Charles "CJ" Johnson
Tyler Kelly
Linda Watanabe McFerrin
Lyle Swallow and Jack Becker
Clayton Whetmore, DO
Ruth Brousseau
Dan Hodges
Rick Kaplowitz
Gayle McGill
Nandini Pal
Alan Parso
Cassidy Poon and John Saluni
W. E. "Wes" Sanders

Index to Waterclolors

Title	Size		Price
Mountain Lion	12 x 16,	framed	$1400
Victorian Abstract I	16 x 20	unframed	550
Honeymoon Home	12 x 16	unframed	550
Heirloom Tomatoes	5 x 6	unframed	75
Kaleidoscopic Sampler	9 x 12	unframed	350
Picking Blueberries	16 x 12	framed	750
Bouquet Series	16 x 12	framed	750
Multi-colored Iris	12 x 9	200 giclée	NFS
Flamenco Dancer	29 x 22	unframed	2000
Fort Hood Bivouac	12 x 16	unframed	450
Creative Energy:	31 x 24	framed	500 giclée, 3000
Destructive Energy	31 x 24	framed	500 giclée, 3000
Picking Strawberries	12 x 9	framed	500
Graceful Sea Images	20 x 16	framed	800
Morris and Skippy in the Hen Yard, a photo			NFS
Hen Hatching Eggs	12 x 16	unframed	550
Land's End, San Francisco	16 x 12	framed	750
Beauty in Darkness	12 x 9	unframed	550
Monet's Garden in Rain	16 x 20	framed	1200
Monet's Garden in Sun	16 x 20	framed	1200
Depression Phase			NFS

Title	Size		Price
My Son Leonard	16 x 12		NFS
Manic Phas	16 x 12		NFS
Leonard's Car Wreck	9 x 12		NFS
Grieving Father	9 x 12		NFS
The Purple Torso	16 x 12	framed	850
Parting Sorrow	16 x 12	unframed	650
Rubber Paradise	12 x 9	unframed	550
Sunshine Rainbow	20 x 16	unframed	900
Angel's Serenade	9 x 12	unframed	350
Temple Mount & Calvary	9 x 12	unframed	350
Fiery Explosion	16 x 12	unframed	750
Burning Ember	16 x 12,	ramed	950
Service Is Sacred	16 x 12	framed	1150
Bound Slave	12 x 16	framed	1150
Leather Flag	30 x 22	unframed	2000
Barque on Stormy Sea	16 x 20	unframed	750
Drying Thistle	12 x 9	unframed	450
Napa Valley Winery	22 x 30	unframed	2000
Victorian Abstract II	16 x 20	unframed	550
Underwater Paradise	22 x 30	unframed	2000
Cable Cars, SF	20 x 16	framed	2000

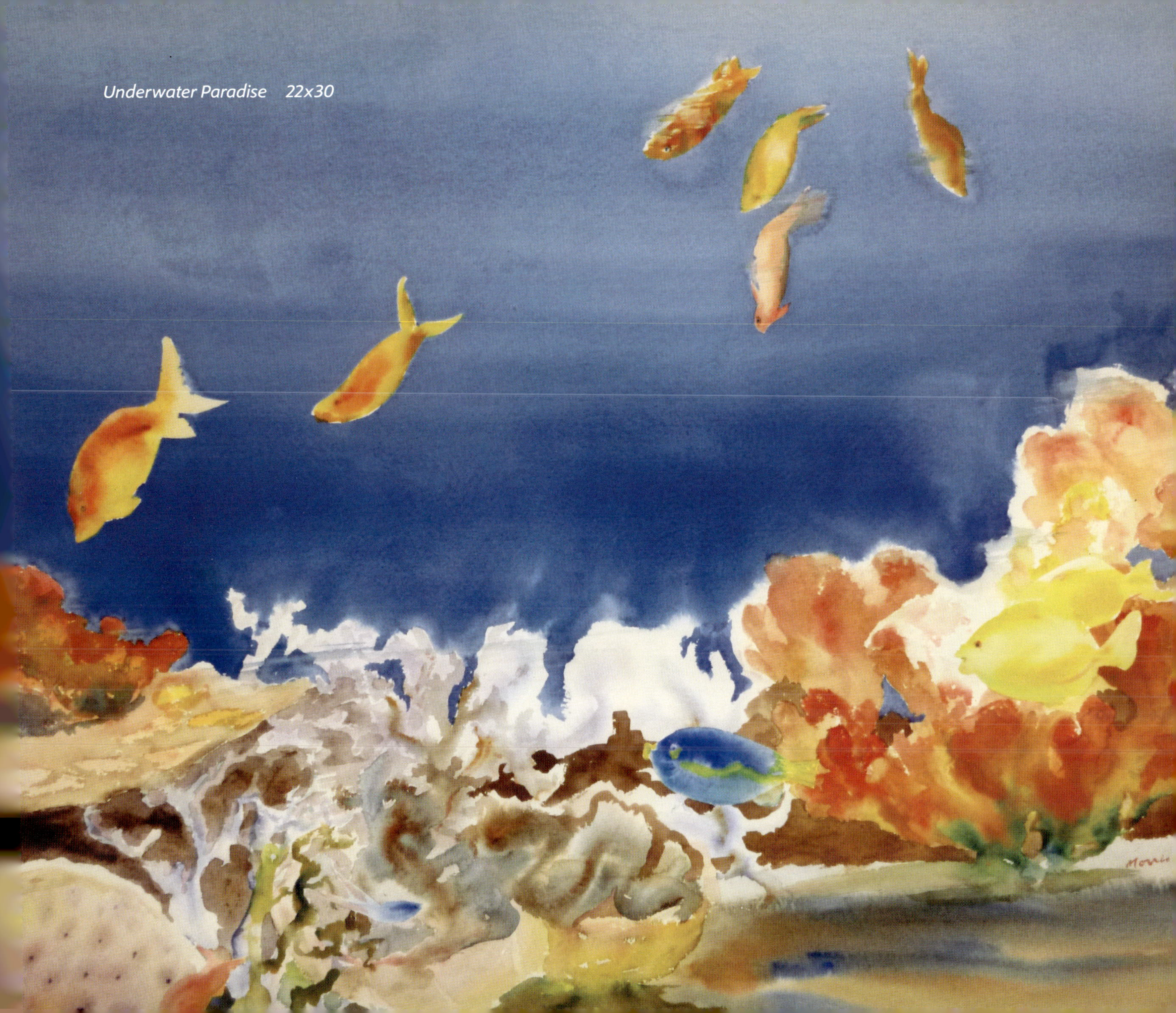
Underwater Paradise   22x30